# Mass Migration in Europe:
# A Model for the U.S.?

# MASS MIGRATION IN EUROPE:

## *A Model for the U.S.?*

### By Robert Spencer

For more information about this book, visit
**SECUREFREEDOM.ORG**

*Mass Migration in Europe: A Model for the U.S.?*
is published in the United States
by the Center for Security Policy Press,
a division of the Center for Security Policy.

ISBN: 9798679603776

The Center for Security Policy
Washington, D.C.
Phone: 202-835-9077
Email: info@SecureFreedom.org
For more information, visit SecureFreedom.org

Book design by Bravura Books

Cover art by Oleg Atbashian

August 26, 2020

# Contents

# CHAPTER 1

## THE CAUSES OF MASS MIGRATION INTO EUROPE

### *A crisis long in the making*

The current crisis in Europe has been brewing for many years. As long ago as 2004, the historian Bernard Lewis told the German newspaper *Die Welt* that "Europe will be Islamic by the end of the century."[1]

Lewis was respected throughout the world as a careful, judicious observer; he was anything but an alarmist or hysteric. And even back in 2004, he had ample reason at that time to come to his conclusion, including:

- Sweden's third-largest city, Malmö, had by 2004 become one-quarter Muslim, and that proportion was rapidly growing. Nor were the Muslims of Malmö inclined to demonstrate their moderation. Even the police were afraid: "If we park our car it will be damaged—so we have to go very often in two vehicles, one just to protect the other vehicle," reported a police officer in Malmö. Meanwhile, Swedish ambulance drivers would not enter some areas of Malmö unless police accompanied them."[2]

- In that same year, the Nordgårdsskolen in Aarhus, Denmark, become the first Dane-free Danish school. The students came entirely from Denmark's fastest-growing constituency: Muslim immigrants.[3]

- Also in Denmark in 2004, the Qur'an became required reading for all upper-secondary school students.[4] There was nothing wrong with that in itself, but given the current ascendancy of political correctness all over Europe, it was no surprise that critical perspectives were not included.

- Pakistani Muslim leader Qazi Hussain Ahmed gave an address at the Islamic Cultural Center in Oslo, Norway. He was readily allowed into the country despite that fact that, according to Norway's *Aftenposten*, he had previously made "flattering comments about Osama bin Laden, and his party, Jamaat-e-Islami, also has hailed al-Qaeda members as heroes."[5] While in Norway, Ahmed declined to answer questions about whether or not he thought homosexuals should be killed.[6]

Around the same time, Dutch officials uncovered at least 15 separate terrorist plots, all aimed at punishing the Netherlands for its 1,300 peacekeeping troops in Iraq.[7] And in Spain, Moroccan Muslims, including several suspected participants in the March 11, 2004, jihad bombings in Madrid, took control of a wing of a Spanish prison in the fall of 2004. From there, they broadcast Muslim prayers at high volume, physically intimidated non-Muslim prisoners, hung portraits of Osama bin Laden, and boasted, "We are going to win the holy war."[8] The guards' response? They asked the ringleaders please to lower the volume of the prayers.

Over and a decade and a half later, nothing has happened that would lead anyone to think that Lewis was wrong. What was happening in 2004 is all the more widespread today. Indeed, by the time Lewis made his statement, it was already far advanced. This advance became sharply more rapid and aggressive after German Chancellor Angela Merkel opened her country's doors to mass migration on August 31, 2015. Speaking at a press conference on that day, Merkel warned, "If Europe fails on the question of refugees, if this close link with universal civil rights is broken, then it won't be the Europe we wished for."[9]

Continuing her moralistic argument, Merkel stated, "Europe as a whole must move. If we don't succeed in fairly distributing refugees, then of course the Schengen question will be on the agenda for many," that is, the open borders between European states. Her seizure of the initiative in this regard led to Germany being inundated with more migrants than other European countries, as 800,000 entered the country in 2015 alone. Merkel seemed to anticipate this as she said, "The world sees Germany as a country of hope and opportunity; that was not always the case." She suggested that opposition to mass migration was an unacceptable moral evil: "There is no tolerance for those who question the dignity of other people."

Merkel summed up her call to Europe with words that became famous and emblematic of the entire enterprise: "We can do it!"[10] As a result of this idealism, Europe today faces numerous problems stemming from its nearly continent-wide policies of mass migration, including migrant enclaves and no-go zones; rising crime rates, especially skyrocketing rates of sexual assault and rape; as well as severe challenges to European culture. Meanwhile, Turkish President Recep Tayyip Erdogan wields mass migration as a weapon to wring concessions out of Europe, often with willing help from European Union officials. This has given rise to a large-scale political movement to end mass migration, which has been tarred unfairly as racist and neo-Nazi, and yet continues to grow, particularly in Central and Eastern Europe.

## *The making of Eurabia*

The long-term implications for Europe could be dire. Yet this crisis was largely the doing not of societal pressures, political unrest, and wars in the Middle East, as was commonly believed. Instead, it was almost solely the responsibility of European leaders and the result of choices they made. When Dutch Prime Minister Mark Rutte's Liberal VVD party emerged victorious in March 2017, Turkish Foreign Minister Mevlüt Çavuşoğlu was enraged despite Rutte's consistent pro-immigration stance and declared, "Now the election is over in the Netherlands. . . . When you look at the many parties, you see there is no difference between the social democrats and fascist [Geert] Wilders. All have the same mentality. Where will you go? Where are you taking Europe? You have begun to collapse Europe. You are dragging Europe into the abyss. Religion wars will soon begin in Europe. Because they were of different faiths, they killed each other 100 years ago. But they learned a lesson from this and the European Union, the Council of Europe was set up."[11]

Çavuşoğlu was partially correct. The European Union wasn't established in order to prevent religious wars; they had already become a thing of the past before it emerged. The EU did, however, enter into a series of agreements with the Arab League that led ultimately to the mass migrant influx of the 21st century. The pioneering historian Bat Ye'or has detailed how the European Union since 1973 has been constructing "a whole infrastructure of alliances and economic, industrial, media, cultural, financial bonds with the countries of the Arab League."[12] This new Euro-Muslim entity—which she dubbed "Eurabia"—has been consciously intended to become "a counterweight to American power" on the world stage, "whose aim was to separate and weaken the two continents by an incitement to hostility and the permanent denigration of American policy in the Middle East."[13]

This massive endeavor began as a simple dialogue between representatives of countries north and south of the Mediterranean. Bat Ye'or explained:

After the Yom Kippur War and the Arab oil blackmail in 1973, the then-European Community (EC) created a structure of Cooperation and Dialogue with the Arab League. The Euro-Arab Dialogue (EAD) began as a French initiative composed of representatives from the EC and Arab League countries. From the outset the EAD was considered as a vast transaction: The EC agreed to support the Arab anti-Israeli policy in exchange for wide commercial agreements. The EAD had a supplementary function: the shifting of Europe into the Arab-Islamic sphere of influence, thus breaking the traditional trans-Atlantic solidarity. The EAD operated at the highest political level, with foreign ministers on both sides, and the presidents of the EC—later the European Union (EU)—with the secretary general of the Arab League. The central body of the Dialogue, the General Commission, was responsible for planning its objectives in the political, cultural, social, economic, and technological domains; it met in private, without summary records, a common practice for European meetings.[14]

As far back as April 1983, in a speech to the Hamburg Symposium's Euro-Arab Dialogue, West German Foreign Minister Hans-Dietrich Genscher delineated the high hopes that West Germany had for the dialogue. Given the dominant influence that West Germany exercised in the European Union (which the united Germany has continued), Genscher's words likely expressed the goals of many people who were in positions of power in Europe:

> The Euro-Arab Dialogue would indeed remain incomplete if the political side were to be ignored or not taken seriously. Both parties to the Dialogue, both partners, should always remind themselves of the joint Memorandum issued in Cairo in 1975, the Charter of the Dialogue. The Memorandum contains the following quote: "The Euro-Arab Dialogue is the outcome of the common political will which strives for the creation of a special relationship between the two groups." We Europeans spoke out in a clear and convinced manner for a revival of the Euro-Arab Dialogue in the Vienna Declaration of June 13, 1980. Since then, the various working groups within the Dialogue have become more active and the prospects for the future are more promising.

> Our Arab partners in the Dialogue have also indicated that they are in favour of continuing and intensifying this Dialogue. Both in the course of this joint venture, our Symposium, and through its outcome, it will become clear that we are determined to give the Euro-Arab Dialogue a new and long lease of life.[15]

Genscher's call was heeded. Bat Ye'or noted, "Europe's economic greed was instrumentalized by Arab League policy in a long-term political strategy targeting Israel, Europe, and America."[16]

After nearly 50 years, Eurabia is now an established political and economic entity. As Bat Ye'or stated,

> Over the years, Euro-Arab collaboration developed at all levels: political, economic, religious and in the transfer of technologies, education, universities, radio, television, press, publishers, and writers unions. This structure became the channel for Arab immigration into Europe, of anti-Americanism, and of Judeophobia, which—linked with a general hatred of the West and its denigration—constituted a pseudo-culture imported from Arab countries. The interpenetration of European and Arab policies determined Europe's relentless anti-Israel policy and its anti-Americanism. This politico-economic edifice, with minute details, is rooted in a multiform European symbiosis with the Arab world.[17]

In exchange for the opening of Arab markets, Europeans encouraged Muslim immigration into Europe, *discouraged* assimilation of these immigrant populations, and fostered the dissemination in Europe of Islamic perspectives on history and contemporary politics. Meanwhile, European foreign policies were brought into harmony with the aims and goals of the Islamic world.

Through a succession of international agreements, Europe agreed to support the Islamic world's political aims—particularly its anti-Israel stance—in exchange for favored treatment in Arab world markets. Observed Bat Ye'or: "From the outset the [Euro-Arab Dialogue] was considered as a vast transaction: the EC agreed to support the Arab anti-Israeli policy in exchange for wide commercial agreements."[18]

The cultural and societal changes that have arisen out of this initiative in Europe have been seismic in scale, but Bat Ye'or explained that

> beyond a fleeting awareness, the overwhelming majority of Europeans and Americans do not understand the new Eurabian entity, which is only the first step in a steady progression toward its Arabization and Islamization. Europe has evolved from a Judeo-Christian civilization, with important post-Enlightenment/secular elements, to a 'civilization of dhimmitude,' i.e., Eurabia: a secular-

Muslim transitional society with its traditional Judeo-Christian mores rapidly disappearing.[19]

This evolution has been the result not of inertia, drift, or gradual decline, but of conscious choices and decisions made at the highest levels. According to Bat Ye'or, "this program of Euro-Arab symbiosis has been codified in a detailed report entitled, 'Dialogue between Peoples and Cultures in the Euro-Mediterranean Area.'" Released in October 2003, "this report (whose contributors included [renowned novelist] Umberto Eco and [influential Islamic spokesman] Tariq Ramadan) was to establish complete interdependence between Europe and the Arab-Muslim world."[20] What was envisioned was independence in every sense of the word, not just a closer economic relationship. The group that was to be established to accomplish this would have extraordinary power:

> Romano Prodi, President of the European Commission, established the High-Level Advisory Group which stated the aims, policies, and routine functions of the foundation. The Advisory Group mandated that the foundation have complete financial and administrative independence in managing its budget and in choosing its partners. In support of this remarkable request, the Advisory Group argued that the foundation needed considerable resources to cover its activities that would be extraordinarily expensive, as they will encompass all the countries of the EU. The Advisory Group further justified such conditions by invoking its lofty aim, which "is nothing less than peace itself." And this "peace"—accomplished through "brotherly love" and "dialogue" between the North and the South of the Mediterranean—will be achieved by a total economic, political, and cultural fusion.[21]

These were not just the empty words of a pro forma agreement that no one took seriously or worked to implement. In the intervening years, that "total economic, political, and cultural fusion" has significantly advanced, with mass migration specifically aiding the cultural fusion. "One can choose to ignore it," Bat Ye'or wrote, "but Eurabia is a tangible entity. Eurabia has a discernible historical development, and its functionaries are now well entrenched in each European parliament, and at the head of the European Commission."[22]

## *Jettisoning Europe's traditional culture*

Bat Ye'or explained that the Euro-Arab Dialogue made explicit provision for what was essentially the jettisoning of Europe's traditional culture:

> A wide-ranging policy was then first sketched out, a symbiosis of Europe with the Muslim Arab countries, that would endow Europe—and especially France, the project's prime mover—with a weight and a prestige to rival that of the United States. This policy was undertaken quite discreetly, outside of official treaties, under the innocent-sounding name of the Euro-Arab Dialogue. An association of European parliamentarians from the European Economic Community (EEC) was created in 1974 in Paris: the Parliamentary Association for Euro-Arab Cooperation. It was entrusted with managing all of the aspects of Euro-Arab relations—financial, political, economic, cultural, and those pertaining to immigration. This organization functioned under the auspices of the European heads of government and their foreign ministers, working in close association with their Arab counterparts, and with the representatives of the European Commission, and the Arab League.

> This strategy, the goal of which was the creation of a pan-Mediterranean Euro-Arab entity, permitting the free circulation both of men and of goods, also determined the immigration policy with regard to Arabs in the European Community (EC). And, for the past 30 years, it also established the relevant cultural policies in the schools and universities of the EC. Since the first Cairo meeting of the Euro-Arab Dialogue in 1975, attended by the ministers and heads of state both from European and Arab countries and by representatives of the EC and the Arab League, agreements have been concluded concerning the diffusion and the promotion in Europe of Islam, of the Arabic language and culture, through the creation of Arab cultural centers in European cities. Other accords soon followed, all intended to ensure a cultural, economic, political Euro-Arab symbiosis. These far ranging efforts involved the universities and the media (both written and audio-visual), and even included the transfer of technologies, including nuclear technology. Finally a Euro-Arab associative diplomacy was promoted in international forums, especially at the United Nations.[23]

This was not just high-sounding rhetoric. When Nicolas Sarkozy became President of France in May 2007, he pressed forward with plans for a "Union for the Mediterranean," which would, he declared, do nothing less than "change the world."[24] This association of European and North African majority-Muslim countries would give North African Muslims an unprecedented voice in the internal policies of Europe and endow their immigrant countrymen in Europe with power and influence beyond their numbers. Sarkozy, for his part, defended the project in terms that recalled Chamberlain speaking about his arrangements for the demise of Czechoslovakia. "Failure," said Sarkozy in April 2008, "would mean taking a terrible responsibility towards our children and all future generations."[25]

## Hostility toward Israel and the U.S.

As a result of these agreements, Europe would move away from its historic allies. Bat Ye'or noted,

> Arab economical ascendancy over the EC influenced the latter's policy toward Israel. The EAD [Euro-Arab Dialogue] was the vehicle for legitimizing the propaganda of the PLO, procuring it international diplomatic recognition, and conferring on Arafat's terrorist movement honor and international stature by supporting Arafat's address to the General Assembly of the United Nations on November 13, 1974. Through the labyrinth of the EAD system, a policy of Israel's delegitimization was planned at both the EC's national and international levels. Approved instructions from the highest political, religious, and academic authorities functioned within the EAD's multiple commissions, implicating the media, universities, and diverse cultural activities. The EAD was the mouthpiece which diffused and popularized throughout Europe the defamation of Israel. France, Belgium, and Luxembourg were then the most active agents of the EAD.[26]

This myopia hasn't only affected Israel. Said Bat Ye'or: "Europe's pathological obsession with the Arab-Palestinian conflict has obscured the criminal ongoing persecution of Christians and other minorities in Muslim lands worldwide, and the sufferings and slavery of millions from jihad wars in Africa and Asia."[27]

As a result of all this, noted Bat Ye'or, Javier Solana, the Secretary General of the Council of the European Union from 1999 to 2009, often "merely parrot[ed] the Arab League's Amr Moussa, or the Palestinian Authority's Yasser Arafat. Hence Solana parrots the pan-Arab refrain that no reforms can be achieved in any Muslim country before the settlement of the Arab-Israeli conflict, reiterating the same fatuous statements made by Amr Moussa."[28]

This began much earlier than the 2003 report: "The EU continues to proclaim that all negotiations must be conducted with Arafat alone and that the Middle East conflict is at the center of world politics. Those two assertions were repeated endlessly at the Fez, Amman, and Taif Summits (1980–81)."[29] The negative effects of this were immense: "The EU's unlimited funds finance anti-Israeli and anti-American campaigns, as well as the 'dialogue' industry. Regarding Israel in particular, it appears as if the EU has become the obsequious mouthpiece of the Arab League."[30] The same tendencies showed in the European Union's relations with the United States:

> Strategically, the Euro-Arab Cooperation was a political instrument for anti-Americanism in Europe, whose aim was to separate and weaken the two continents by an incitement to hostility and the permanent denigration of American policy in the Middle East. The cultural infrastructure of the EAD allowed the traditional cultural baggage of Arab societies, with its anti-Christian and anti-Jewish prejudices and its hostility against Israel and the West, to be imported into Europe. The discredit heaped on the infidel Judeo-Christian culture was expressed by the claim of the superiority of the Islamic civilization, at which source European scholars, over the centuries—it was said—had humbly slaked their thirst for knowledge.[31]

Despite its being a sharp departure from the perspectives and values that had built Europe itself, Bat Ye'or observed, the Eurabian initiative had made massive inroads into Europe:

> Drowned in this wave of Arab cultural and religious expansionism that was integrated into the cultural activities of the EAD, Europeans adopted the Arab-Islamic conception of history. The obsequiousness of certain academics, subjected to a political power dominated by economic materialism, is reminiscent of the worst periods of the decline of civilizations. The suppression of intellectual freedom imported from undemocratic Muslim countries, attached to a

culture of hate against Israel, has recently led to the exclusion and
boycott of Israeli academics by some of their European colleagues.[32]

By now, these attitudes are firmly entrenched. "This Eurabian ethos," she
stated, "operates at all levels of European society. Its countless functionaries,
like the Christian janissary slave-soldiers of past Islamic regimes, advance a
jihadist world strategy. Eurabia cannot change direction; it can only use
deception to mask its emergence, its bias and its inevitable trajectory.
Eurabia's destiny was sealed when it decided, willingly, to become a covert
partner with the Arab global jihad against America and Israel."[33]

What is happening in Europe today is simply the playing-out of
these agreements.

# CHAPTER 2

## MIGRANT ENCLAVES AND NO-GO ZONES

### *Fox News' apology and the reality of the situation*

Given the cultural aspects and implications of the Eurabia imperative, it is not surprising in the least that Europe would now feature, in many countries spanning almost the entire continent, enclaves where a culture and societal system prevail that were not until recently considered European at all. In many areas of Europe, there are growing areas where police officers, firefighters, and other emergency personnel are not welcome and are sometimes even attacked if they dare to venture in.

These have been popularly termed "no-go zones" and have by that label frequently been dismissed as a hysterical fantasy of right-wing zealots. Yet the dismissals are often based on straw-man definitions of what constitutes a "no-go zone" in the first place. The claim is advanced that those who warn about the advent of no-go zones in Europe are asserting that in these areas, there are no non-immigrants, or no non-Muslims, and everyone who lives there is from another country, and another culture and societal order prevail.

In reality, this is only partially true, at best. The reality of European no-go zones is not that they contain no non-immigrants or non-Muslims, or that the law enforcement officers or other personnel of the state in question cannot go there at all. Rather, in these areas, there is a significant and often a majority non-indigenous population, and the laws of the land often take a back seat to the laws and mores of the immigrant group. Police, firefighters, and emergency personnel can enter, but they are not often treated with respect.

These areas have been developing in Europe for many years and began to receive attention from public figures and the media well over a decade ago.

The very existence of these enclaves, however, has also been the subject of immense controversy. In January 2015, Fox News issued an apology for statements made on the air by terror expert Steve Emerson and others about Muslim no-go zones in Britain and France. However, the apology didn't say what it has widely been reported as saying—and there was considerable evidence that Muslim areas in both countries are a growing law enforcement and societal problem.

Fox Report host Julie Banderas stated,

> Over the course of this last week we have made some regrettable errors on air regarding the Muslim population in Europe, particularly with regard to England and France. Now, this applies especially to discussions of so-called "no-go zones," areas where non-Muslims allegedly aren't allowed in and police supposedly won't go.

> To be clear, there is no formal designation of these zones in either country and no credible information to support the assertion there are specific areas in these countries that exclude individuals based solely on their religion.

> There are certainly areas of high crime in Europe as there are in the United States and other countries—where police and visitors enter with caution. We deeply regret the errors and apologize to any and all who may have taken offense, including the people of France and England.[34]

The establishment media reaction to this demonstrated that the idea that no-go zones did not exist was taken for granted among the media elites. The *Atlanta Journal-Constitution*'s joyous headline read: "Fox News admits 'no-go zones' are fantasy."[35] The far-left Crooks and Liars blog exulted: "Fox Pundits Finally 'Apologize' After a Week of Being Mocked for 'No Go Zones' Claim."[36] The *New York Times* stated as fact its opinion that no-go zones did not exist: "Fox News Apologizes for False Claims of Muslim-Only Areas in England and France."[37] The leftist media has seized on Fox's apology to declare that there are aren't any no-go zones in France or Britain—and by extension that there is no problem with Muslim populations in Europe. *NewsHounds*' summation was typical: "Fox News has become the laughingstock of Europe this week as first England and then France lampooned its ignorant, Islamophobic reporting."[38]

The only problem with all the mockery of Fox News on this point was that there was a problem with Muslim areas in Europe—and the Fox apology didn't actually go so far as to say there wasn't. To be sure, the controversy began with undeniably inaccurate statements from Emerson. He said on Fox on January 11, 2015, that "there are actual cities like Birmingham that are totally Muslim, where non-Muslims just simply don't go in."[39] That was false, and Emerson acknowledged that and apologized.

However, Emerson was not guilty of fabrication, just of overstatement. Some of the comments on a piece in the UK's *Daily Mail* about his gaffe and British Prime Minister David Cameron's reaction to it (he called Emerson a "complete idiot") insisted that Emerson was at least partially right [spelling, grammar, and punctuation as in the originals]: "Just shows cameron doesn't even know what is happening in this country , as the news presenter is totally correct , its a no go zone ."[40] "There ARE some parts of Birmingham where you darent or shouldn't go !"[41] "Is he far off the truth? Maybe it's not true for Birmingham as a whole but there are certain areas where it is true. Certainly it is true of certain other Towns in the UK. Bradford, Leicester, Luton spring to mind."[42]

What's more, as long ago as April 2008, the Rt. Rev. Michael Nazir-Ali, Anglican Bishop of Rochester in England, warned that Islamic jihadists were turning "already separate communities into 'no-go' areas where adherence to this ideology has become a mark of acceptability." He declared that non-Muslims

> may find it difficult to live or work there because of hostility to them and even the risk of violence. . . . Attempts have been made to impose an 'Islamic' character on certain areas, for example, by insisting on artificial amplification for the Adhan, the call to prayer. Such amplification was, of course, unknown throughout most of history and its use raises all sorts of questions about noise levels and whether non-Muslims wish to be told the creed of a particular faith five times a day on the loudspeaker.[43]

Indeed. It also raised questions about the supremacist agenda of those operating the loudspeakers. But no public debate on Islamic supremacism was forthcoming; instead, Nazir-Ali's words provoked a furor in Britain. Muslims furiously denied that what the bishop said was true and directed their ire against him. One Muslim leader, Mohammed Shafiq of the Ramadhan Foundation, fulminated, "Mr. Nazir-Ali is promoting hatred towards Muslims and should resign."[44]Nazir-Ali began to receive death threats and was placed under police protection.[45] Yet his words received indirect confirmation from the British government in March 2008 when officials actually forbade British military personnel to wear their uniforms in certain parts of the country in order to prevent them from being abused by "ethnic minorities."[46] And what

Nazir-Ali reported was no surprise: an undercover investigation in British mosques by Britain's Channel 4 *Dispatches* program in late 2006 found Muslim preachers exhorting audiences to create a "state within a state" in Britain. One preacher, Dr. Ijaz Mian, exclaimed, "You cannot accept the rule of the kaffir [unbeliever]. We have to rule ourselves and we have to rule the others."[47]

Fox's apology was carefully worded to acknowledge this reality and did not, in fact, rule out the existence of no-go areas. It concentrated on the fact that they had not received official acknowledgment: "To be clear, there is no formal designation of these zones in either country and no credible information to support the assertion there are specific areas in these countries that exclude individuals based solely on their religion.[48]

That says as much as it says and no more. It says that neither the British nor the French government has designated any areas to be no-go zones where non-Muslims aren't allowed in, and that there is no evidence that non-Muslims are not allowed into any areas in either country.

But this carefully worded statement does not actually say that there aren't areas in Britain or France in which non-Muslims are menaced for not adhering to Islamic law. That is a real and abundantly documented problem. Emerson pointed to it when he said, "In parts of London, there are actually Muslim religious police that actually beat and actually wound, seriously, anyone who doesn't dress according to Muslim, religious Muslim attire."[49]

## Sharia zones in London

While Emerson's implication that this was an ongoing phenomenon was incorrect, there were indeed such Sharia enforcers in London between 2011 and 2013. In July 2011, the *Daily Mail* reported: "Islamic extremists have launched a poster campaign across the UK proclaiming areas where Sharia law enforcement zones have been set up. Communities have been bombarded with the posters, which read: 'You are entering a Sharia-controlled zone—Islamic rules enforced.'"[50]

In December 2013, members of one of these self-styled "Muslim patrols" were imprisoned; according to one report, in London, they "harassed people, berating them with shouts of 'this is a Muslim area!' They forced men to dump their alcoholic drinks, instructed women on the appropriate way to dress, and yelled insults at those they perceived to be gay."[51]

They didn't just berate people; as Emerson said, they beat them. In YouTube videos, they threatened to do so, saying: "We are coming to implement Islam upon your own necks."[52] In June 2013, Muslims attacked an American who was drinking on the street, grabbing the bottle out of his hands and smashing him in the eye with it, causing permanent injury.[53] In August 2013, according to the *Daily Mail*, "two brothers in law who went on a sponsored walk wearing comedy mankinis had to be picked up by police—after they were pelted with stones and eggs by residents who told them 'this is a Muslim area' and demanded they leave."[54]

A "Muslim area"—maybe even a "no-go zone." Not in the sense that non-Muslims are barred from entering, but in that, if they do enter, they have to adhere to Sharia restrictions.

In Bradford, England, meanwhile, councilors warned that the advent of no-gone zones was leading the city "toward disaster."[55] Arshad Hussain, Bradford Council's Corporate Overview and Scrutiny Committee chairman, noted in December 2017 that while crime was increasing, many Bradford residents were "scared to speak up in case they caused offence" regarding the "many areas of this city" that had become dangerous for the native population.[56] Another Bradford councilor, Vanda Greenwood, observed that young "Asian" men—the British codeword for "Muslim"—were making women feel unsafe. "There is a real problem of people's perception of Bradford," said Greenwood. "My daughter is 23 and she and her friends say they will not come into Bradford for a drink or night out because they say there are gangs of Asian males hanging around."[57]

Arshad Hussain added the telling observation that "Community relations in this city were a lot better 25 years ago. Are we really achieving what we are supposed to be achieving? I don't think so." He added: "Last month on Bonfire Night in my ward, three pubs were stoned by Asian youths. These were the only white businesses in the area. No Asian businesses were attacked. They were targeted because they were white. I am really cheesed off with things like this. There are so many areas in this city where white people are scared to go into. Likewise, there are other areas where Asian people are scared to go into."[58]

## No-go zones in France

The Fox apology was all the more curious in light of the fact that others, even on the left, had noticed the no-go zones in France years before some Fox commentators began talking about them in the wake of the Charlie Hebdo attacks. David Ignatius wrote in the *International Herald Tribune* in April 2002 about the suburbs of Paris, "Arab gangs regularly vandalize synagogues here, the North African suburbs have become no-go zones at night, and the French continue to shrug their shoulders."[59]

*Newsweek*, hardly a conservative organ, reported in November 2005 that "according to research conducted by the government's domestic intelligence network, the Renseignements Generaux, French police would not venture without major reinforcements into some 150 'no-go zones' around the country–and that was *before* the recent wave of riots began on Oct. 27."[60]

The police wouldn't venture into these areas without major reinforcements in 2005. After another decade and a half of misplaced tolerance and fear of confrontation on the part of French officials, there is no reason to believe that the situation in these areas has improved for people who do not share the now-dominant religion and culture.

And on January 8, 2015, the day after the jihad massacre at the offices of the satirical magazine Charlie Hebdo in Paris set off Fox's discussions of no-go zones in France, the *New Republic* wrote, "The word *banlieue* ('suburb') now connotes a no-go zone of high-rise slums, drug-fueled crime, failing schools and poor, largely Muslim immigrants and their angry offspring."[61]

Terrorism analyst Daniel Pipes reported back in November 2006 that there were no fewer than 751 areas in France that were euphemistically classified as "Sensitive Urban Zones" (ZUS). Pipes explained that these were actually "places in France that the French state does not control," and that "a more precise name for these zones would be Dar al-Islam, the place where Muslims rule."[62] European historian and journalist Paul Belien noted in January 2008 that

> the ZUS are centers of drug trafficking. . . . Since they operate from within the ZUS the drug dealers are beyond the reach of the French authorities. The ZUS exist not only because Muslims wish to live in their own areas according to their own culture and their own Shariah laws, but also because organized crime wants to operate without the judicial and fiscal interference of the French state. In France, Shariah law and mafia rule have become almost identical.[63]

Police were under virtual siege in some of these no-go zones in France, to the extent that the government of South Korea warned Korean tourists in February 2017 not to visit the Paris suburb of Seine-Saint-Denis, which was dominated by Muslim migrants. The advisory was issued after migrants assaulted and robbed a South Korean tourist group while it was stuck in a traffic jam, then set fire to their tour bus. Jean-François Zhou, President of the Chinese Association of Travel Agencies in France, stated that "increasingly violent" assaults and robberies of this kind were transforming France, once one of the most popular tourist destinations in the world, into "one of the worst destinations for foreign tourists."[64]

With the same dangers in mind, in December 2016, the Paris public transport company RATP entered a partnership with a tech firm to create a mobile phone app, "Mon Chaperon" (My Chaperone), that alerted users to criminal activity taking place in areas to which or through which they would be traveling. The app also allows travelers to match up with others making similar journeys so they can avoid being targeted by criminals on public transit. The app's developer, Fabien Boyaval, explained, "I had this idea after one of my friends was assaulted in the street in Montpellier."[65] It is noteworthy that his idea did not involve police, but rather, travelers taking care of each other.

In 2018, after a drastic increase in crimes committed by Muslim migrants from Morocco, 1,600 people living in the Goutte d'Or area of Paris, which was home also to a massive population of migrants, petitioned the French government for help in dealing with the young migrants who were terrorizing the non-Muslim residents. In response, the government sent Moroccan police officers to Goutte d'Or, apparently in the belief that authorities from their home country could more effectively rein in the migrants than French police could.[66] It was testimony to the disrespect many of the migrants held for the authorities in the European countries where they had settled and the impotence of those authorities in dealing with the difficulties the migrants created: all they could do was outsource the problem.

Clearly, there was and is a massive problem in these areas. The Charlie Hebdo cartoonists were murdered for blaspheming against Islam. Two of the three Charlie Hebdo murderers were born and raised in France. Where did they get their ideas about killing blasphemers? Not from French schools. They learned them in the Muslim areas where they were born and raised. What's more, France leads the West in the number of Muslims who have traveled from there to wage jihad for the Islamic State, with well over a thousand Muslims leaving France to join the caliphate. Where did they get their understanding of Islam?

The French government has objected to claims that these areas are outside their control and subject to Sharia, but it is obvious that whatever control they do have over these areas is not enough to prevent the indoctrination of all too many young Muslims into the jihad ideology.

There needs to be a balanced, honest public discussion of these Muslim areas in Britain and France. The need for such a discussion has only grown in the intervening years. And Britain and France are by no means alone.

## No-go zones in Sweden

The same situation has prevailed in Sweden, where young migrants have on more than one occasion called emergency services not because there was an emergency, but so that the migrants could attack them. In the Swedish city of Malmö, which is home to an enormous concentration of Muslim migrants, migrant youths set fire to two cars and then pelted firefighters who came to put out the fires with rocks and bottles. The firefighters had to retreat, whereupon the young migrants burned down a building. Young migrants in no-go areas have also attacked emergency medical personnel.[67]

By September 2016, three Swedish police officers were quitting every day. Police Sergeant Peter Larsson declared, "We have a major crisis. Many colleagues have chosen to leave. We will not be able investigate crimes, we have no time to travel to the call-outs we are set to do. A worsened working environment means that many colleagues are now looking around for something else."[68] He ascribed the widespread dissatisfaction among police to a deteriorating work environment: "The violence against us in the police and the paramedics and firefighters, has become much worse. We're talking about stone throwing, violence, fires. It has become much worse in recent years."[69]

A Swedish resident of a no-go zone in Gothenburg, Tina Svensson, explained that while violence was increasing, police were frequently nowhere to be found. In a recent incident, she said, "there were two guys who were shot. With some kind of automatic weapons. Two magazines, perhaps. It may not be what you would expect when you are out walking the dog."[70]

The no-go zones were an increasing drain on the resources of the municipalities involved. Swedish authorities began constructing a new police station in Stockholm's Rinkeby no-go zone. But in August 2018, masked assailants drove a car into the station, which had not yet been completed, and then set their car, which was filled with fireworks, on fire.[71]

In light of such incidents, it was understandable that police would continue to quit their jobs. Officials in many notorious no-go zone areas were forced to spend money on private security guards to make at least some effort to stem the rising tide of migrant crime. In Stockholm, which featured no-go zones not only in Rinkeby, but also in Tensta, Husby, and Järva, officials spent 70 million Swedish kronor (over $7 million) on these guards.[72]

These guards were much needed. The Swedish National Council for Crime Prevention (Brå) released a survey in November 2017 revealing that 48% of the native Swedish residents of Malmö believed that it was too dangerous to go out at night. In the Swedish city of Ystad, 58% of Swedes revealed that they were deeply worried about skyrocketing crime rates, which were largely due to the migrants. In Stockholm and Gothenburg, the survey results were much the same.[73]

## No-go zones in Germany

Sweden had never experienced all this until it opened its doors to mass migration. And the situation was the same elsewhere in Europe: in March 2019 in Germany, researcher Ralph Ghadban identified no-go zones in the Berlin areas of Kottbusser Tor, the Tiergarten, and Neukölln. These were, according to Ghadban, "dangerous areas, so-called no-go areas, in which Arab clans have the upper hand. . . . No-go areas are a law-free area. Policemen are persecuted, besieged, and harassed. Policewomen are groped. They receive threats from clan members such as 'we know where you live' or 'we know where your children go to school', but they are usually empty threats."[74] Usually, but not always.

Understandably, police in many areas of Germany, as in Sweden, are completely demoralized and are leaving their jobs. In 2011, a former chief police commissioner in Germany, Bernhard Witthaut, said,

> Every police commissioner and interior minister will deny it. But of course we know where we can go with the police car and where, even initially, only with the personnel carrier. The reason is that our colleagues can no longer feel safe there in twos, and have to fear becoming the victim of a crime themselves. Even worse: in these areas, crimes no longer result in charges. They are left to themselves.[75]

Despite such testimony, however, the controversy about whether no-go areas even existed has continued. Political leaders and law enforcement officials across Europe generally denied or downplayed their existence. In the Altenessen area of the German city of Essen in October 2016, one citizen told the mayor and police chief: "I was born here and I do not feel safe anymore."[76] Instead of being sympathetic and detailing a plan of action, however, Police Chief Frank Richter said, "I'm sick of it"—that is, of hearing how dangerous the city had become because of the migrant influx.[77] Essen's Lord Mayor Thomas Kufen dismissed complaints as well, saying: "Altenessen is not a no-go area, the people here are just angry."[78]

German Chancellor Angela Merkel, however, was unusually forthright in a February 2018 interview. She acknowledged that "no-go areas" did indeed exist in Germany, saying, "there are such spaces, and you have to call that by name and you have to do something about it." She even stated, "Of course, the arrival of so many refugees has raised multiple questions," without pointing out that it was her government that had worked so assiduously to bring them in. Merkel assured the German public that in connection with these no-go zones, she had their safety in mind: "It's always a point to me that [ensuring] domestic security is the state's obligation, the state has the monopoly of power, the state has to make sure that people have the right to it whenever they meet and move in a public space."[79]

When she made those statements, however, Merkel was embroiled in a contentious reelection campaign, in which mass migration was a key issue. Her statements did not turn out to herald any reversal of her open-door policies.

## No-go zones in other European countries

In other European countries as well, citizens have looked in vain to governments for help.

*Deutsche Welle* TV discovered a no-go zone in September 2007 in the Molenbeek neighborhood of Brussels, when a local Muslim leader threatened them and denied that they had a right to film in that area. Of this man, *Deutsche Welle* remarked, "Belgian laws do not interest him. The man is confident that it is he who controls the neighborhood." It continued, "Many police officers are afraid that the State no longer wields authority here—at least not the sole authority. They know that Islamists view Molenbeek as subject only to Muslim law."[80]

Yet despite all this coming to light, nothing has been done, and the no-go areas have continued to grow. There are still zones of this kind all over Europe.

# CHAPTER 3

## MIGRANTS AND CRIME

### *A new crime wave*

In the first half of 2016, migrants in Germany, who were overwhelmingly Muslim, committed 142,500 crimes, an average of 780 every day. This was a significant increase from 2015, during which migrants committed 200,000 crimes.[81] Yet on August 31, 2016, one year to the day after she opened Germany's doors to the refugee influx of 2015, Germany's Merkel assured her people that all would be well: "Germany will remain Germany, with all that we hold most precious and dear," she said. "So many refugees want to come to Germany or Austria or Sweden because they are treated well here, according to our values and principles. This is reflected in our constitution and our laws, our liberty, our democracy, in our overwhelming commitment to a social market economy. All this will not change."[82]

Yet even aside from jihad terror activity, Muslim migrants have also been largely responsible for a rise in crime rates in general. After a wave of migrant crime in Denmark, in September 2017, trying to curb the growing power of migrant gangs, Danish police issued a warning that young men between the ages of 17 and 25 should stay away from public areas of Copenhagen. Preben Bang Henriksen, a spokesman for Denmark's ruling party—Venstre, Denmark's Liberal Party—was aghast at the rapid deterioration of public safety, and stated, "We have not had such warnings from the police since the Second World War. It is totally unacceptable."[83] Meanwhile, Trine Bramsen of the opposition Social Democrats called the skyrocketing crime rates in Denmark a "catastrophe."

Officials in some European countries, however, aware that they are responsible for the migrant influx, have done their best to obscure this fact. In December 2019, a report from Sweden's Linköping University charged the Swedish Crime Prevention Council (Brå) with pressuring its employees to "change findings which, for political, ideological or other reasons, were not desirable. ... If results were not liked, then there was censorship, organisation of results, dimming of results, and highlighting other parts of a study that were not as sensitive or could show a positive result."

## *Denial and obfuscation*

The results that were not wanted involved migrant crime; one report showing evidence of the migrant crime wave was spiked entirely for that reason. In doing all this, the Swedish authorities did what they could to cover their tracks. The Linköping University report stated, "Both interviews and what happened during the data collection indicate that there seems to be a culture of silence within Brå and there seems to be an effort to hire people who are perceived as easy to control." One of the authors of the report, Malin Wieslander, explained that all the report's sources within Brå had been kept anonymous for fear of official reprisals: "Of course, it would have been better if we could have been completely open. But because individuals in this study are so vulnerable, we have chosen to protect them."[84]

Those who were responsible for the migrant influx perpetrated the same coverup in the Netherlands. In May 2019, Dutch Asylum Minister Mark Harbers resigned over a report about migrants and violent crime in which key data were "hidden," particularly about the numbers of migrants who were suspected of murder and rape.[85] Instead of listing those crimes as such, the report grouped them together in an "Other" category that led some Dutch MP's to charge deliberate obfuscation. "I am not only responsible in terms of the law, but I feel responsible," said Harbers, but according to Dutch News, he also charged that the problem went higher up, asserting that "the ministry had been warned not to come up with a top 10 crimes for which asylum seekers were suspects."[86]

When MPs confronted Harbers about why the Asylum Ministry had not given full or precise information about exactly how many "refugees" were involved in criminal activity, Harbers responded that Ministry employees were concerned that this information could cause "confusion."[87] Dutch News reported some of the alarming data that the Asylum Ministry report had attempted to bury: "Last week's report showed 'fake' asylum seekers who come from so-called safe countries, namely Morocco and Algeria, were responsible for almost half the 4,600 incidents requiring police intervention. While most cases involved shoplifting or pickpocketing, police also registered cases of physical abuse, threatening behaviour and a further 1,000 incidents listed as 'other.'"[88] That total included "79 potential sex crimes, including 47 cases of sexual assault, five allegations of child abuse and four alleged rapes plus a string of other violent offences."[89]

## Blaming the Right

In Germany, the denial was even thicker. A revealing incident took place during a parliamentary session in January 2020, when an opposition German MP, Gottfried Curio of the Alternative for Germany (AfD) party, which opposes mass migration, asked Angela Merkel,

> Madame Chancellor, on the recent violence in Augsburg, where a group of young migrants killed one man and seriously injured another—this wasn't a terror attack, but a spontaneous outbreak of violence, which doesn't make it better. Actually, it's worse, because it makes it more commonplace. The perpetrators of Augsburg were born there and in the second generation are living according to the typical norms of internalized machismo. They see it as honorable and strong to exercise violence. Such people turn the public space into a place of fear, a place where the fist rules. So much for the integration fairy tale. The Federal Report on Immigrant Crime shows that Augsburg is the tip of the iceberg. The immigrant perpetrators have multiplied dramatically since 2014. Last year, hundreds of cases of murder and manslaughter, thousands of cases of sexual assault, tens of thousands of cases of bodily injury. In light of such numbers, of migrant criminals, would you speak of isolated incidents, or do you recognize that there are systemic problems?[90]

Merkel replied with the practiced non-answer of a polished political operative:

> First of all, I recognize that a terrible crime was committed in Augsburg and that naturally our thoughts are with the relatives and also with those who were injured. Secondly, I recognize that the government is called upon to combat all forms of violence wherever they occur. We are also working to constantly improve our opportunities for action, for example by creating a large number of new positions in the fight against right-wing extremism. Of course, we are also working in other areas, and we will of course continue this work, but overall I believe our constitutional state is capable of acting at both the federal and state levels.[91]

At Merkel's mention of "right-wing extremism," many of the MPs began laughing. The Augsburg attackers were not "right-wing extremists," but

Muslims, the children of migrants; Merkel's reference to "right-wing extremism" in connection with them was a peculiar manifestation of the fact that the German government was ready and willing to attack the problem of violence from "right-wingers," but not from Muslim migrants or those who had been born and raised in the milieu of no-go zones and the rampant contempt in them for law enforcement and government authorities.

Curio persisted, confronting Merkel:

> From 2014 to 2018, there were over 800,000 immigrant crimes, and these are just the solved ones. Including the estimated unreported cases, there are millions of crimes that could have been prevented by border security. Do you recognize that you are personally at fault for the continued intake of this high-risk group of young male migrants having an Islamic and clan culture? It was and still is completely unnecessary, because this occurs via self-admittance permitted on the basis of an alleged emergency situation, which is now being used for a permanent resettlement. Do you recognize your personal responsibility?[92]

Merkel was, of course, not going to be pinned down so easily. She responded,

> The Federal Chancellor is always responsible for the political events in the country. I'm also glad that I am allowed to hold such an important office. Secondly, there are different views regarding what happened in 2015 and in the following years. I believe that Germany has helped a great many people in need, that society as a whole has made an effort to do so, and that we have also, of course, worked and will continue to work on the order and management of migration, and the figures show that this work is not in vain, but that it has been successful.[93]

The Chancellor's reference to "right-wing extremism" made clear what kind of "order and management of migration" she had: the crushing of dissent from her agenda, rather than an end to, or even slowing of, the migrant influx into Germany. In this, she was not at all alone among German politicians. Even during the coronavirus crisis in April 2020, the Minister of Justice and Anti-Discrimination in Berlin, the Green Party's Dirk Behrendt, argued that Germany should admit the Muslim migrants crowded onto the Greek island of Lesbos, saying, "We have a lot of vacant hotels in Berlin that could also be used to accommodate refugees. We have capacities. The fact that the people of Lesbos live in makeshift tents in the rain and cold is unworthy of the European Union."[94]

The fact that some of the migrants would almost certainly make life more difficult and uncomfortable for native Germans didn't seem to trouble Behrendt, or Merkel, at all. Nor did it haunt the dreams of many other Western European leaders.

## *The Cologne attacks*

As Gottfried Curio noted, the migrant influx was accompanied by a sharp rise in the rates of sexual assault in many countries. Muslim migrants in Europe have also been responsible for an appalling epidemic of rape, sexual assault, theft, petty crime, and looting.

On New Year's Eve, 2015, Muslim migrants committed as many as 2,000 mass rapes and sexual assaults in the German cities of Cologne, Dusseldorf, Dortmund, and Bielefeld, as well as in Stockholm and other major European cities.[95] Muslims from France and Belgium traveled to Cologne to participate in the assaults, after being called to the city on social media.[96] One officer in Cologne recounted that the attackers showed a lack of respect for the police "like I have never experienced in my 29 years of public service."[97] One attacker crowed, "I'm a Syrian! You have to treat me kindly! Mrs. Merkel invited me."[98]

New Year's Eve sex assaults by Muslim migrants were also reported in Finland, Sweden, Switzerland, and Austria.[99] In Sweden, a Muslim migrant stabbed a 15-year-old boy to death because he was trying to shield a girl from sexual assault.[100] In Finland, Ilkka Koskimaki, deputy chief of police in Helsinki, declared, "This phenomenon is new in Finnish sexual crime history. We have never before had this kind of sexual harassment happening at New Year's Eve."[101]

Such assaults weren't limited to that day alone; Sweden has been called the "rape capital of the world" because of the notorious activities of Muslim migrants.[102] Muslim migrants have made Malmö, once a peaceful city, crime-ridden and hazardous.[103]

In Sweden, Muslim migrants from Afghanistan are 79 times more likely to commit rape and other sexual crimes than native Swedes. Migrants and refugees commit 92% of rapes in Sweden. Rapists in Sweden come from Iraq, Afghanistan, Somalia, Eritrea, Syria, Gambia, Iran, Palestine, Chile, and Kosovo, in that order; rapists of Swedish background do not exist in sufficient numbers to make the top ten, and all the nations on that list except Chile and Eritrea are majority Muslim.[104]

In response to the massive number of sexual assaults in her city, Cologne Mayor Henriette Reker vowed to make sure that women changed their behavior so that they didn't provoke the migrants to commit sexual assault again.

Reker said, "The women and young girls have to be more protected in the future so these things don't happen again."[105] She didn't mean protected by police. "This means," Reker continued, "they should go out and have fun, but they need to be better prepared, especially with the Cologne carnival coming up. For this, we will publish online guidelines that these young women can read through to prepare themselves."[106]

Reker's words recalled a hadith in which Muhammad, the prophet of Islam, said to a Muslim woman, "'O Asma, when a woman reaches the age of menstruation, it does not suit her that she displays her parts of body except this and this,' and he pointed to her face and hands" (Sunan Abu Dawud 4092). The idea behind a woman covering everything except her face and hands is rooted in the assumption that if a man is tempted by her, it's her fault. She can therefore try to quell that temptation by removing its impetus and covering up. If she fails to do so, or if she covers up and is attacked anyway, the fault lies entirely with her, and her family can cleanse itself of the dishonor she has brought upon them by putting her to death.

There was no room in this web of assumptions, which remains all too common in the Islamic world, for the idea that if a man rapes or sexually assaults a woman, he bears the guilt. The guilt is all on his victim.

And so Henriette Reker showed the world yet again that when multiculturalism and feminism come into conflict, multiculturalism always wins—at least when it comes to Islam. Feminists have been telling the world for decades that it is outrageous and wrong to say that a rape victim was "asking for it" because of the way she was dressed. But Reker essentially said just that: if only the women in Cologne had been properly "prepared," if only they had had access to her "guidelines," then all would have been well. Reker said nothing about getting Muslim migrants "prepared" for life in Germany, and has made no announcement about issuing any "guidelines" for them about how to keep themselves from molesting women.

For Reker, as for Islamic supremacists everywhere, the responsibility to prevent sexual assault lies solely with them women. What, then, would her "guidelines" direct the non-Muslim women of Cologne to do? If she had been consistent, they would have told women to buy a niqab. Buy a burqa. Or at very least to "dress modestly." In any case, the "guidelines" reminded women that if they were attacked by migrants, it was their own fault, as they should have been more careful.

And so Cologne's Mayor slipped without any evident hesitation into the Sharia mindset that it is entirely the woman's responsibility to avoid tempting men, and entirely her fault if she is attacked.

## *A daily occurrence*

Even before the migrant influx, while on a speaking tour in Germany in 2011, I was told by the 16-year-old daughter of one of the event organizers that she was routinely harassed on the way to school: Muslims on the commuter trains would call her a "whore" and a "slut" because her hair and arms were not covered. This happened, she said, every day.

Sexual assaults by Muslim migrants became, if not a daily occurrence, then a regular feature of life in Germany. One of the migrants who came to Germany from Afghanistan in 2015 and lived on the edges of society, with four different aliases, in September 2018 met an 11-year-old girl. The migrant was 22. "I just asked her," the young migrant recounted at his trial in 2020, "if she wanted to have sex with me."[107] She agreed, and they met a total of three times for sex. The girl's mother stated, "She was a happy girl before. After that, no more."[108] The girl became suicidal.

What had become an all too common occurrence in Germany was an incident that was reported laconically by the Brandenburg police on January 30, 2020:

> The police were called to Tschirchdamm on Wednesday evening. A young man is said to have come too close to two children there. When the officers arrived on the scene, they were able to meet both the teenagers and the adult suspect. According to the girls, the suspect first grabbed them by the buttocks and then held a lighter over their heads. In addition, the man, in broken German and with gestures, apparently made them understand that he wanted to set them on fire. The two girls were then placed in the care of their parents and interviewed by criminologists. At the same time, the 22-year-old suspect, an Afghan, was taken into custody by the Brandenburg Police Department. After they had clarified his identity

there without a doubt and he underwent identification checks, he was released today. The criminal police are now investigating charges of sexual harassment and threats against the 22-year-old.[109]

German officials generally covered up these crimes. The UK's *Express* reported in January 2016 that "Angela Merkel's government is under increasing pressure to come clean over the true numbers of sex crimes linked to migrants after it emerged that authorities deliberately withheld the nationalities of the Cologne attackers for several days. They also 'covered up' similar incidents in other cities including Dusseldorf and Hamburg, Munich and Berlin."[110] Cologne's police chief, Wolfgang Albers, was ultimately fired for covering up the sex assaults in that city.[111]

Similarly, police in the Swedish city of Östersund warned women not to go out by themselves after dark. Regional police chief Stephen Jerand explained, "Now the police are going out and warning women against travelling alone in the city. We have seen a worrying trend. This is serious, we care about the protection of women and that is why we are going out and talking about this."[112]

To her credit, Östersund Mayor Ann-Sofie Andersson took umbrage at this, saying, "The solution can never be to not go out because of such a warning. We have very many women who work in home and social care at night for example. What are they supposed to do?"[113] And Johan Hedin of Sweden's Centre Party declared, "It's wrong if it calls on women to adapt to the criminals. It risks leading people the wrong way, if the victims must adapt to the perpetrators."[114]

## The UK: Muslim rape gangs

The phenomenon of Muslim rape gangs in Britain, and the unwillingness of law enforcement officials to prosecute them for fear of being tarred with charges of "racism," is hardly summed up by the word "scandal." This wasn't just a scandal, it was a surrender—a cultural and societal collapse unprecedented in human history.

*The Guardian* reported in October 2014 that "sexual exploitation of vulnerable children has become the social norm in some parts of Greater Manchester."[115] The denial and obfuscation about why this was happening, however, was thicker than ever: in the very same sentence in which it broke this terrible news, *The Guardian* stated that this phenomenon was "fuelled by explicit music videos and quasi-pornographic selfies, an MP has warned."[116] The MP in question, former social worker Ann Coffey, issued a report on the sexual exploitation of children in Britain that she said would "make painful reading for those who hoped that Rochdale was an isolated case."[117] It was in Rochdale that a group of Muslims were involved in a large-scale sex trafficking ring involving young non-Muslim girls.[118]

Why was this happening, and on such a massive scale? According to *The Guardian*, it was all because social workers and others in positions of authority just didn't like troubled young people: "Coffey said police, social workers, prosecutors and juries are often inherently (albeit unconsciously) prejudiced against vulnerable teenagers—perhaps explaining why, out of 13,000 reported cases of major sexual offences against under-16s in the past six years in Greater Manchester, there have been only 1,000 convictions."[119]

Social workers, prosecutors, and juries were inherently prejudiced against vulnerable teenagers? With that, Coffey could have won the prize for the most preposterous evasion ever offered to try to exonerate Islamic doctrine from responsibility for the evils done by those who acted upon that doctrine regarding non-Muslim women—although she would face stiff competition.

In reality, social workers were not prejudiced against vulnerable teenagers; they had dedicated their lives to aiding people such as vulnerable teenagers. No, what social workers, in the U.S. as well as in Britain, were prejudiced against was being called "racist." In the British town of Rotherham, Muslim gangs brutalized, sexually assaulted, and raped over 1,400 young British girls, while authorities remained extremely reluctant to say or do anything in response, for fear of being labeled "racist."[120] Rotherham officials "described their nervousness about identifying the ethnic origins of perpetrators for fear of being thought as racist; others remembered clear direction from their managers not to do so."[121]

And what were the ethnic origins of those perpetrators? *The Guardian* report didn't mention it (which in itself was telling), but 75%, and probably more (since it was so politically unacceptable to report such things) of these rape and sexual exploitation gangs were "Asian," which is British Newspeak for "Muslim."[122]

Yet despite the continuing horror of these revelations, all too many Britons continued to take it all with equanimity, for to resist it would be "racist" and "Islamophobic." If Ann Coffey and others who were horrified at these rape gangs and the exploitation of children really wanted to stop this practice, they were going to have to stop kidding themselves and their supporters and confront the politically correct elites who hurled such charges at anyone who ventured any criticism of Islam. For the unpleasant truth was that these rape gangs had become "the norm" in all too many cities in Britain because Muslims were taking seriously material from the Qur'an and Sunnah that justified those practices. That fact, however, was too much for the British establishment to handle.

The BBC reported in March 2015 that "South Yorkshire Police knew hundreds of young girls were making claims of sexual abuse in Sheffield but did not act, an ex-police officer has alleged."[123] The tally of these abused girls was beyond belief: in February 2015, the Mirror reported that "there could be up to a million victims of child sexual exploitation in the UK, it is feared."[124]

Even after multiple revelations about rape gang activity and the prosecutions and convictions of many gang members, the rape gang activity continued. According to official figures released in December 2019, over 18,700 children had fallen prey to grooming and rape gangs in Britain during the previous year. This was up from some 15,000 victims in 2014.

These findings were so alarming that some warned of an "epidemic" of such activity.[125] Yet some who had long worked against the gangs charged that the actual number of victims was even higher. Labour MP Sarah Champion declared that the figures showed that the sex gangs remained "one of the largest forms of child abuse in the country."[126] She criticized the government for its failure to respond: "Too many times, government has said it will 'learn lessons', yet 19,000 children are still at risk of sexual exploitation. The government has singularly failed to tackle this issue head on. Its approach has been piecemeal and underfunded."[127]

One reason for this was revealed by former Home Secretary Sajid Javid, when he noted that the perpetrators included a "high proportion of men of Pakistani heritage."[128]

The same scenario played out in cities and towns all over Britain. The mother of one rape gang victim noted that South Yorkshire Police "would not listen and left you in dangerous situations, letting people do what they wanted and they never questioned anybody about what was happening."[129] She called for prosecution of South Yorkshire Police officials (which as of this writing has not been undertaken): "They've always been complicit in what happened, we've seen perpetrators get done, so why are they any different? They've aided and abetted abuse."[130] One South Yorkshire Police official even told this victim's father that the perpetrators could not be prosecuted because of who they were: "With it being Asians, we can't afford for this to be coming out."[131] The official also observed that the rape gangs had been operating freely in Britain for 30 years.

There certainly was a racial component to the rape gang activity. Some Muslim rape gang members referred to their victims as "filthy white girls," "easy meat," and "white trash" and blamed them for their own victimization as uncovered infidels.[132] Even "the wives of convicted Muslim rape gang groomers have said that the young white girls targeted by their husbands are "filthy" and to blame for their own abuse. One of the wives of a jailed rapist said about the victims: "Filthy. How they dress. They have no shame, no fear of Allah."[133]

The official reluctance to rein in the activities of Muslim migrant rape gangs was repeated in many areas all across the country. One possible clue as to why this happened was revealed in March 2020, when Gordon Brown, who was Prime Minister of Britain and leader of its far-left Labour Party from 2007 to 2010, was accused of making a dirty deal with Saudi interests that resulted in a hands-off order to British police regarding the Muslim rape gangs that have plagued the once-sceptered isle for years.

The UK news site Politicalite reported that "during Gordon Brown's short tenure as Prime Minister he borrowed money from the Saudi's [sic]—but the deal had BIG strings attached."[134]

Politicalite quoted an anonymous source that it said was connected to the world of finance, claiming, "In return for the money, the condition they insisted on, was that Muslims in Britain must be free to do anything they like."[135]

Whether it was because of Brown or for some other reason, there was no doubt that British authorities for years were notably unwilling to do anything about the rape gangs, despite the fact that thousands of British girls' lives were destroyed. The police stood down because they were told to do so. Politicalite "reported in 2018 that ex-North West Chief prosecutor alleged that the Home Office ordered police to ignore grooming gang claims in 2008—though Home Secretary Jacqui Smith had nothing to do with the order."[136] The news site also noted that Nazir Afzal, who "successfully prosecuted the notorious Rochdale rape gang told the BBC in 2018 that in 2008 the Home Office sent a circular email to all police forces calling on them to not investigate the sexual exploitation of young girls in towns and cities across the UK."[137]

Said Afzal: "You may not know this, but back in 2008 the Home Office sent a circular to all police forces in the country saying 'as far as these young girls who are being exploited in towns and cities, we believe they have made an informed choice about their sexual behaviour and therefore it is not for you police officers to get involved in.'"[138]

Twelve years later, the same reluctance to face this problem still prevailed. In January 2020, the UK's *Daily Mail* reported that according to a "damning" new report, "sex attacks on young girls by Asian grooming gangs were ignored by police fear of stoking racial tensions."[139]

Yet that report did not appear. In February 2020, British Home Secretary Priti Patel charged officials of the Home Office with "obfuscation" regarding a promised but much-delayed report on the ethnicity of the rape gangs.[140] Her predecessor as Home Secretary, Sajid Javid, had ordered the report back in July 2018, but as the perpetrators were almost completely Pakistani Muslims, the publication was delayed; then it was announced that the findings would not be published at all, but merely reviewed within the Home Office itself. According to a Home Office source, Patel was being "given the run around by officials" who were "not being completely up front about this."[141] Yet the need for the report was urgent: "The reason we need offender profiles is to allow the police to disrupt and prevent grooming gangs. We have this data on other forms of child abuse, why not this?"[142]

The answer was obvious: because the perpetrators were in the main from groups that British officials did not wish to portray in any kind of negative light.

Nor was this reluctance anything new. Britain's Birmingham Mail reported in November 2014 that Birmingham's City Council buried a report about Muslim cab drivers exploiting non-Muslim girls back in 1990. A researcher, Dr. Jill Jesson, drafted a report on this issue. But, she explained, "the report was shelved, buried, it was never made public. I was shocked to be told that copies of the report were to be destroyed and that nothing further was to be said. Clearly, there was something in this report that someone in the department was worried about."[143]

Authorities were worried because Jesson's report illustrated that virtually all of the exploitative cab drivers were "Asians," and their victims were "white," i.e., non-Muslim. The exploitation of these girls stems from Qur'an-based religious beliefs, but British officials were terrified because stopping this exploitation would appear "racist."

Jesson elaborated:

> There was a link between the sexual abuse of the girls and private hire drivers in the city. I thought at the time I did the work that there was an issue with race. Most of the girls were white. I was asked to take this link out, to erase it. . . . Every time a news item has come on about sexual grooming of young girls and girls in care, and the link, too, between private hire drivers, I have thought "I told them about that in 1991 but they didn't want to acknowledge it."[144]

"The sad part of this story," Jesson concluded, "is not the suppression of evidence but that the relevant organisations have failed to address this problem."[145]

What kind of society was willing to allow up to a million of its young girls to be pressed into service as sex slaves and prostitutes by predatory gangs? What kind of society declined to hunt down, prosecute, imprison, and deport more than a small number of these gang members because its guardians of law and justice knew that the leftist establishment would accuse them of racism, bigotry, and Islamophobia, and bring them to certain professional ruin, if they dared try to bring these men to justice?

## *The treatment of Tommy Robinson*

An indication of how powerful that establishment was, and how determined it was not to let the full truth of the rape phenomenon be known, was the case of Tommy Robinson.

On August 1, 2018, Tommy Robinson was ordered freed from a stint in prison that he never should have been serving in the first place. The *New York Times* reported that Robinson was "arrested in May after he live-streamed a video from outside a criminal trial in Leeds, England, which had a news media blackout, revealing the defendants' identities. He was sentenced to 13 months in prison for contempt of court, provoking an international outcry in far-right circles."[146] Those "far-right circles" had good reason to be concerned. The *Times* continued, "On Wednesday, the Court of Appeal ordered his release, pending a new hearing in his case. The court questioned the speed with which he had been tried and convicted, noting that it took five hours from the time of his arrest to a conviction."[147]

Indeed, Tommy Robinson had been arrested, tried, and sentenced with a Stalinist rapidity for the crime of calling attention not only to the Muslim rape gang crisis in the UK, but to the abject failure of British officialdom to deal adequately with that crisis, for fear of being charged with "racism" and "Islamophobia."

He was freed in August 2018, but later he was ordered to return to prison again, once again giving the impression that Britain was becoming a police state in which it was illegal to criticize Islam and mass Muslim migration in Britain today.

That impression was underscored by the treatment Robinson received in prison in 2018. Canadian journalist Ezra Levant reported on August 3, 2018, that "Tommy was physically and psychologically abused in prison. You can see it in his face. His appearance is shocking—he lost 40 pounds of weight in just two months. If he were to have stayed in prison much longer, I fear his very life would have been in danger."[148]

"I'm not a victim, I'm a target," Robinson said in an interview with Levant, and explained: "What they tried to do was to mentally destroy me. That wasn't a prison sentence, that was mental torture."[149]

The treatment of Tommy Robinson in prison was as unconscionable as it was consistent with the British government's determination to crush all resistance to its program of mass Muslim migration and capitulation to Sharia supremacists. The treatment of Tommy Robinson in prison was a demonstration of pure police state tactics. Meanwhile, the establishment media defamed him as "far-right" and as a "white nationalist," despite the fact that Robinson's extensive record of activism substantiated neither charge.

## *Light sentences*

The same reluctance to address the problem of rape gangs manifested itself elsewhere in Europe in a curious leniency toward the perpetrators who were prosecuted. On March 31, 2020, a Finnish court handed down its sentences for eight men, all of whom were Muslim, who had been convicted of repeatedly raping and abusing a girl who was only 12 years old when the abuse began. One of the perpetrators, Hassan Mohamud Mohamed, received a four-and-a-half-year sentence; another, Abdo Ibrahim Ahmed, got four years and two months. Three others, Quassar Mohsin Sbahi Aldhulaie, Rahmani Gheibai, and Ali Osman Mohamed, were given four years. The lightest sentence was given to Shiraqa Yosef, who got two years.[150]

Meanwhile, in Belgium in February 2020, a 33-year-old Muslim migrant from Afghanistan who was publicly identified only as Irfanullah M. got eight months in prison for sexually assaulting a 16-year-old girl on a train in January 2019. Even this light sentence was too much for the perpetrator, who said to the judge: "I know nothing. I have a wife and children. I have never done anything bad. Can I appeal?"[151]

The brevity of these sentences was remarkable and suggested that the same reluctance to cast Muslim migrant communities in a negative light that prevailed in Britain was also prevalent in Finland. The fear of appearing "racist" was compounded by the fear of appearing to be religiously intolerant.

## *Why it happened*

No one in Britain or elsewhere in Europe had the courage to admit that rape gang members committed their evil acts not because they were "Asians," but rather because the perpetrators believed their religion gave them the right. And these cover-ups proceeded from a fear that non-Muslims would begin to have negative views of Islam as a result.

A case could be made that the perpetrators are correct in their view, which may explain why the rape gang activity was so prevalent, and why rape gang members were overwhelmingly Muslim. The Qur'an teaches that infidel women can be lawfully taken for sexual use (cf. its allowance for a man to take "captives of the right hand," 4:3, 4:24, 23:1–6, 33:50, 70:30). The Qur'an says, "O Prophet, tell your wives and your daughters and the women of the believers to bring down over themselves of their outer garments. That is more suitable that they will be known and not be abused. And ever is Allah Forgiving and Merciful" (33:59). The implication there is that if women do not cover themselves adequately with their outer garments, they may be abused, and that such abuse would be justified.

Not all Muslims, of course, engaged in this activity or thought it justified according to Islamic tenets, but those who did could find ample justification in Islamic teaching. A victim of one of these Muslim rape gangs said that her rapists would quote the Quran to her and believed their actions were justified by Islam.[152] Thus, it came as no surprise when Muslim migrants in France raped a girl and videoed the rape while praising Allah and invoking the Qur'an.[153] And the victim of an Islamic State jihadi rapist recalled, "He told me that according to Islam he is allowed to rape an unbeliever. He said that by raping me, he is drawing closer to God.... He said that raping me is his prayer to God."[154]

All of that is still ignored, and the Muslim rape gangs went unreported, unprosecuted, and in general unstopped because those who called attention to them were demonized as "Islamophobic," "hateful," and "bigoted."

## *Official silence*

In the Goutte d'Or no-go zone of Paris, women were harassed on a regular basis by Muslim migrants from Morocco. One woman noted in July 2018 that the migrants even barred women from entering some of the neighborhood cafes, adding, "These are insults, incessant reflections. The atmosphere is agonising, to the point of having to modify our itinerary, our clothes. Some even gave up going out."[155] Paris officials tried to deal with the problem by establishing programs that would keep young migrants from congregating in the streets all day with nothing to do, but the migrants showed scant interest in joining.

Yet hardly anything was said about all this in the public forum. In the summer of 2016, Krystyna Pawłowicz, a member of the Polish parliament, charged German authorities with attempting to "cover up the crimes of their Arab guests, or even shift the blame upon themselves."[156] There was also evidence that migrant crimes were being covered up in the Netherlands and Sweden as well.[157]

The justification for these mass rapes and assaults that is provided in the Qur'an has never been discussed in the establishment media, or at any governmental level in any country. Yet such a discussion could have important implications for how to persuade migrants to stop behaving in this manner, and for judging how easy it will be to do so. But this discussion cannot be had: it's Islamophobic. Feminists have been completely indifferent, even though what women face in Europe is far more serious than the plight of women in the U.S. today. Fear of being labeled an Islamophobe apparently trumps even feminism's core concerns. American and European liberals concerned about "Islamophobia" should consider the implications for their own daughters.

# CHAPTER 4

## MIGRANTS AND TERRORISM

W hile there is no doubt some of the refugees were grateful for the hospitality they were shown, others clearly were not. The most obvious indicator of this was the involvement of Muslim refugees in jihad terror activity. All of the Islamic jihadis who murdered 138 people and wounded over 400 others in Paris in a series of jihad attacks in November 2015 were refugees who had recently been welcomed into Europe.[158] After the attacks, the Islamic State issued a statement claiming responsibility for them, and warning,

> Let France and all nations following its path know that they will continue to be at the top of the target list for the Islamic State and that the scent of death will not leave their nostrils as long as they partake in the crusader campaign, as long as they dare to curse our Prophet (blessings and peace be upon him), and as long as they boast about their war against Islam in France and their strikes against Muslims in the land of the Caliphate with their jets, which were of no avail to them in the filthy streets and alleys of Paris. Indeed, this is just the beginning. It is also a warning for any who wish to take heed.[159]

So war was declared, and acts of war carried out—and the response has been drearily predictable. *Salon* published a piece entitled, "Our terrorism double standard: After Paris, let's stop blaming Muslims and take a hard look at ourselves," and another entitled, "And so the hate speech begins: Let Paris be the end of the right's violent language toward activists."[160] *The Guardian* worried that after the Paris jihad murders on Friday, "far-right groups may well fuel more hatred."[161] Neither *Salon* nor *The Guardian*, nor any other mainstream media outlet, published any realistic assessment of the advancing jihad threat in France and the West in general.

German Interior Minister Thomas de Maizière, meanwhile, was swift to try to dissociate the Paris attacks from the migrant influx into Europe: "I would like to make this urgent plea to avoid drawing such swift links to the situation surrounding refugees."[162] Unfortunately for de Maizière, there was the inconvenient fact that the attackers were "refugees."

In de Maizière's own country, the situation was no better. Germany's domestic intelligence agency admitted in July 2017 that hundreds of jihadis had entered the country among the refugees, and that 24,000 jihadis were active in Germany.[163]

In a similar vein, France's President Emmanuel Macron has declared that climate change is the most serious threat that France faces today. In December 2018 in the French city of Strasbourg, however, a Muslim named Cherif Chekatt reminded Macron that France faces another threat, one that could prove to be immensely more serious: jihad. Chekatt opened fire at a Christmas market in his native Strasbourg, murdering four and injuring 11.[164]

Chekatt's attack followed a series of failures by law enforcement officials. He was "on a list of 'security threats,'" France's "Fiche S" list of people who pose a serious terror threat. RT reported that the regional prefecture announced, "The author of these acts, listed as a security threat, had been sought by police" on the day of the attack, but they hadn't been able to catch up with him before he opened fire.[165] Even worse, a former London police inspector, Peter Kirkham, explained that there were too many jihadis to keep track of: "There are so many people that are involved around the edges of this sort of terrorism if this is what it turns out to be, that you can't keep any sort of meaningful surveillance on them. Even just monitoring the use of communications and social media would be too much."[166]

Britain's senior counterterrorism officer, Metropolitan Police Assistant Commissioner Neil Basu, said the same thing in February 2020. The sheer scale of the challenge meant that officers needed the public's help to stop future terror attacks. "With 3,000 or so subjects of interest currently on our radar and many convicted terrorists soon due to be released from prison," he said, "we simply cannot watch all of them all the time."[167] Basu added, "Part of the solution must be ensuring those who pose the greatest threat to our society are removed from it, and so my colleagues and I are supportive of the Government's plans to strengthen our ability to keep the most dangerous terrorists locked up for longer."[168]

Even that, however, would not get to the root of the problem, particularly as more migrants with values radically different from those of British society continue to stream into the country.

## A call to terror attacks in Europe (and America)

Europe's leaders had reason to be more troubled than they were. On September 21, 2014, Islamic State (ISIS) spokesman Abu Muhammad Adnani issued a lengthy and remarkable statement calling Muslims in the West to jihad. The West, he said, was not as strong as it seemed to be: it was, rather, "a conceited and brash encampment of falsehood, which demonstrates itself to be powerful, and subduing, one that no conqueror can dominate nor any defender withstand. But the reality is they are fearful and terrified, humiliated and left with a weak plan, shaken and defeated, despite their uninhibited movement throughout the lands."[169]

By contrast, the believers were weak in earthly wealth and military might but had the power of Allah on their side—an ironic proclamation given the fact that most Western analysts dismissed ISIS as entirely un-Islamic. He said that "the followers of the messengers"—that is, the prophets—have "lower numbers, meager equipment, and a weaker voice." Nonetheless, "their strength can never be subdued. Their authority can never be broken. They are firm in every battle. And they are forefront in every encounter, having neither fear nor dread. In the end, they will have the triumph and victory." Why? Because of "their faith in Allah, the Mighty, the Compeller. From Him is their strength, and through Him is their authority. He is sufficient for them, and upon Him they rely. They are certain of His aid. And they returned having attained His favor and bounty. They do not fear anyone save Him."[170]

Adnani told the "soldiers of the Islamic State: "By Allah, He has healed the chests of the believers through the killing of the nusayriyyah (Alawites) and rafidah (Shiites) at your hands."[171] This was a reference to the Qur'an's promise that Allah would soothe the hearts (or "heal the chests" as Adnani put it, and "satisfy the breasts" in this translation) of those who waged jihad against the unbelievers: "Fight them; Allah will punish them by your hands and will disgrace them and give you victory over them and satisfy the breasts of a believing people and remove the fury in the believers' hearts" (9:14–15).

Comparing the skepticism that greeted the Islamic State's declaration of the caliphate to the skepticism that greeted Muhammad, Adnani declared, "If the people belie you, reject your state and your call, and mock your caliphate, then know that your Prophet (blessings and peace be upon him) was belied. His call was rejected. He was mocked."[172] But, he said, Allah would grant the Islamic State victory because of its fidelity to him.

Then came the warning: "O America, O allies of America, and O crusaders, know that the matter is more dangerous than you have imagined and greater than you have envisioned." Like many other jihadists, he boasted that the Muslims would defeat the infidels because they loved death more than the infidels loved life, and since Paradise awaited them, they won either way: "You fight a people who can never be defeated. They either gain victory or are killed. And O crusaders, you are losers in both outcomes, because you are ignorant of the reality that none of us is killed but to resurrect the dead amongst us." He said that if a jihadist "survives, he lives as a victor with freedom, might, honor, and authority. And if he is killed, he illuminates the path for those after him and goes on to his Lord as a joyful martyr."[173]

This made, said Adnani, for an invincible fighting force:

> O crusaders, you have realized the threat of the Islamic State, but you have not become aware of the cure, and you will not discover the cure because there is no cure. If you fight it, it becomes stronger and tougher. If you leave it alone, it grows and expands. If Obama has promised you with defeating the Islamic State, then Bush has also lied before him.[174]

Adnani also predicted a dark future for the U.S. and Europe—partially at the hands of the Muslims in the West:

> O Americans, and O Europeans, the Islamic State did not initiate a war against you, as your governments and media try to make you believe. It is you who started the transgression against us, and thus you deserve blame and you will pay a great price. You will pay the price when your economies collapse. You will pay the price when your sons are sent to wage war against us and they return to you as disabled amputees, or inside coffins, or mentally ill. You will pay the price as you are afraid of travelling to any land. Rather you will pay the price as you walk on your streets, turning right and left, fearing the Muslims. You will not feel secure even in your bedrooms. You will pay the price when this crusade of yours collapses, and thereafter we will strike you in your homeland, and you will never be able to harm anyone afterwards. You will pay the price, and we have prepared for you what will pain you.[175] . . .
>
> You must strike the soldiers, patrons, and troops of the tawaghit [rebels against Allah]. Strike their police, security, and intelligence

members, as well as their treacherous agents. Destroy their beds. Embitter their lives for them and busy them with themselves.

If you can kill a disbelieving American or European—especially the spiteful and filthy French—or an Australian, or a Canadian, or any other disbeliever from the disbelievers waging war, including the citizens of the countries that entered into a coalition against the Islamic State, then rely upon Allah, and kill him in any manner or way however it may be.

Do not ask for anyone's advice and do not seek anyone's verdict. Kill the disbeliever whether he is civilian or military, for they have the same ruling. Both of them are disbelievers. Both of them are considered to be waging war [the civilian by belonging to a state waging war against the Muslims]. Both of their blood and wealth is legal for you to destroy, for blood does not become illegal or legal to spill by the clothes being worn. The civilian outfit does not make blood illegal to spill, and the military uniform does not make blood legal to spill.

The only things that make blood illegal and legal to spill are Islam and a covenant (peace treaty, dhimma, etc.). Blood becomes legal to spill through disbelief. So whoever is a Muslim, his blood and wealth are sanctified. And whoever is a disbeliever, his wealth is legal for a Muslim to take and his blood is legal to spill. His blood is like the blood of a dog; there is no sin for him in spilling it nor is there any blood money to be paid for doing such.[176]

The weapon didn't matter, only the outcome:

If you are not able to find an IED or a bullet, then single out the disbelieving American, Frenchman, or any of their allies. Smash his head with a rock, or slaughter him with a knife, or run him over with your car, or throw him down from a high place, or choke him, or poison him. Do not lack. Do not be contemptible. Let your slogan be, "May I not be saved if the cross worshipper and taghut (ruler ruling by manmade laws) patron survives." If you are unable to do so, then burn his home, car, or business. Or destroy his crops.

If you are unable to do so, then spit in his face. If your self refuses to do so, while your brothers are being bombarded and killed, and while their blood and wealth everywhere is deemed lawful by their enemies, then review your religion. You are in a dangerous condition because the religion cannot be established without wala' [loyalty to believers] and bara' [disavowal of unbelievers].[177]

## Anti-Semitism

While Adnani called for targeting all "unbelievers" across Europe, Jews have been the favored targets of the new migrants. Accordingly, Jews are threatened in Europe to an extent they have not been since the days of Hitler. And it's getting worse by the day. According to the English journalist Ambrose Evans-Pritchard, in Antwerp, "Arab gangs have been preying on Hassidic children as they walk to school, forcing those identifiable as Jewish to move around with escorts."[178]

According to Omer Taspinar, a visiting fellow at the Brookings Institution, "The perpetrators of anti-Semitic incidents in France are not right-wing extremists protecting the 'French race' from Jewish contamination: The 400 or so anti-Semitic incidents documented in the country during 2001 have mostly been attributed to Muslim youth of North African origin."[179] Some of these attacks were particularly damaging. On March 30, 2002, "masked assailants smashed stolen cars into a synagogue in Lyon before setting them ablaze. A witness said a group of approximately 15 youths stormed the building. No one was injured in the incident, but the synagogue was destroyed."[180] A synagogue in Marseille was burned the same weekend, after surviving a Molotov cocktail attack the previous fall.

In May 2002, Mohamed Latreche, the founder of the French Muslims' Party (PMF), "held a rally in Strasbourg with Hamas and Hezbollah representatives, at which flyers were handed out calling for boycotts of Israeli, American, and British products. Those with Jewish owners were marked with the Nazi yellow star and the German word Jude."[181] Early in 2003, a Paris rabbi was stabbed in the stomach not long after receiving "a threatening letter referring to Jihad—the Muslim holy war—against enemies of the Palestinians."[182]

Another victim was a 15-year-old named Jérémy Bismuth, who "was attacked by a group of other children, mostly Muslim, at the private Catholic school he then attended. They dragged him into the school's locker room showers shouting that they were going to gas him as the Nazis had gassed Jews. He was beaten and flogged with a pair of trousers whose zipper scratched one of his corneas."[183]

On March 31, 2017, Mundhir Abdallah, an imam in Copenhagen, was filmed preaching a Friday sermon at the al-Faruq Mosque in which he quoted a notorious statement attributed to Muhammad, the prophet of Islam, saying that the Last Day "will not come unless the Muslims fight the Jews and the Muslims kill them."[184]

Abdallah was not referring to a twisted, hijacked version of the true, peaceful Islam. The saying of Muhammad to which he referred is found in a collection of hadith, reports on Muhammad's words and deeds, that Islamic scholars consider to be authentic. It depicts Muhammad saying,

> Abu Huraira reported Allah's Messenger (may peace be upon him) as saying: The last hour would not come unless the Muslims will fight against the Jews and the Muslims would kill them until the Jews would hide themselves behind a stone or a tree and a stone or a tree would say: Muslim, or the servant of Allah, there is a Jew behind me; come and kill him; but the tree Gharqad would not say, for it is the tree of the Jews.[185]

In all too many Islamic teachings and traditions, Jews are the villains of the piece. The Qur'an depicts the Jews as inveterately evil and bent on destroying Muslims' wellbeing. They are the strongest of all people in enmity toward Muslims (5:82), fabricate things and falsely ascribe them to Allah (2:79; 3:75, 3:181), claim that Allah's power is limited (5:64), love to listen to lies (5:41), disobey Allah and never observe his commands (5:13), dispute and quarrel (2:247), hide the truth and mislead people (3:78), stage rebellion against the prophets and reject their guidance (2:55), are hypocritical (2:14, 2:44), give preference to their own interests over the teachings of Muhammad (2:87), wish evil for people and try to mislead them (2:109), feel pain when others are happy or fortunate (3:120), are arrogant about their being Allah's beloved people (5:18), devour people's wealth by subterfuge (4:161), slander the true religion and are cursed by Allah (4:46), kill the prophets (2:61), are merciless and heartless (2:74), never keep their promises or fulfill their words (2:100), are unrestrained in committing sins (5:79), are cowardly (59:13–14), are miserly (4:53), are transformed into apes and pigs for breaking the Sabbath (2:63–65; 5:59–60; 7:166), and more.

Abdallah also hailed the coming caliphate, the single unified state of the Muslims worldwide, and said that it would wage jihad in order to liberate Jerusalem "from the filth of the Zionists," and by so doing, "the words of the Prophet Muhammad will be fulfilled."[186]

Dan Rosenberg, a leader of Copenhagen's Jewish community, was understated when he said, "We are concerned weak and impressionable people may perceive this kind of preaching as a clear call to violence and terror against Jews."[187] Also boding ill for the future was the fact that Abdallah's words were not taken amiss by the worshippers at the al-Faruq Mosque. A reporter from Denmark's TV 2 went to the mosque on May 11, 2017, and spoke to worshippers there for two hours. But he wasn't able to find anyone who would denounce the genocidal anti-Semitism of Mundhir Abdallah.[188]

One Muslim at the mosque said of Abdallah, "I do not think he's hurting anything."[189] Another tried to convince the reporter that Islam forbids killing but did not address the clear call to kill in Abdallah's words. Denmark's Immigration and Integration Minister, Inger Støjberg, noted correctly, "Had this happened in a Danish folk church, then there would have been people in the congregation who stood up and protested."[190] Of Abdallah's words, Støjberg remarked, "This is completely preposterous, undemocratic and awful."[191]

But neither Inger Støjberg nor anyone else seemed able or willing to do anything effective to prevent further "preposterous, undemocratic and awful" statements from being made, and even worse, to prevent Muslims from acting upon them. And they were: Italian journalist Giulio Meotti noted in March 2017 that "the European Union Agency for Fundamental Rights revealed that a third of the Jews of the Old Continent has stopped wearing religious symbols because of fear of attacks. The president of the Jewish Consistory of Marseille, Zvi Ammar, asked the Jews 'not to wear the yarmulke in the street so as not to be recognized as Jews.'"[192]

In one sadly typical incident, a 14-year-old Jewish student at the Friedenauer Gemeinschaftsschule in Berlin was driven out of the school by repeated threats and beatings from Muslim students. "I loved the fact that the school was multicultural . . . the kids and teachers were so cool," the boy recalled.[193] But after he enrolled in November 2016, things quickly went wrong: once he mentioned that he was Jewish, everything changed. "First my Turkish friend Emre said he could no longer hang out with me because I was Jewish. Then other pupils started saying stereotypical things about how Jews only want money and hate Muslims."[194]

The Muslim students began to abuse him verbally, and then to beat him. "This boy, Jassin, whose parents are Palestinian, asked me if I'm from Israel. I've never been to Israel. He said Palestine will burn Israel and his friends said Turkey will burn Israel. He kept kicking me. One day he came up to me from behind and he punched me in the back. I became dizzy ... I had a bruise for a week or two. Every time something bad happened, I told myself I could manage it, but it only got worse."[195] The beatings became a daily occurrence.

The boy's family was appalled: they had chosen the school because of its large number of immigrant students and had themselves recently hosted a Syrian refugee in their home. But their multicultural bona fides were of no avail, and they pulled their son out of the school. The Central Council of Jews in Germany called the boy's treatment at the school "anti-Semitism of the ugliest form."[196] Aaron Eckstaedt of the Moses Mendelssohn Jewish High School in Berlin, said that Jewish parents frequently contacted him to transfer their children to his school "in reaction to anti-Semitic statements coming overwhelmingly from Arabic or Turkish classmates."[197]

The situation has deteriorated to the extent that in Paris, according to Meotti, "Jews are advised to 'walk in groups,' never alone." Accordingly, "40,000 Jews have left France in the last fifteen years, one-tenth of the whole French population. In the tolerant, liberal and democratic West, where Muslim minorities have become more and more assertive, Jews have become more and more 'invisible.' The European Jewish Congress has publicized a shocking poll: 'A third of the European Jews think of emigrating.' That is 700,000 people."[198]

European authorities, predictably, are doing what they can to keep this quiet. On April 4, 2017, a Muslim named Kobili Traore entered the apartment of one of his neighbors, a 66-year-old Jewish woman named Sarah Halimi. While screaming "Allahu akbar" and calling Halimi "Satan" and "Dirty Jew," he began to torture her, and ultimately threw her out of her apartment window to her death.[199]

Two months later, 18 prominent French citizens, including historian Georges Bensoussan and philosopher Alain Finkielkraut, joined Frédérique Ries, a member of the European Parliament from Belgium, to lodge a public protest of the fact that the Paris Prosecutor's Office did not charge Traore with a hate crime and did not mention anti-Semitism in his indictment.

"French authorities," said Ries, "have treated her murder with icy silence. No national mobilization for Sarah, she died as the media remained quasi-indifferent."[200] She pointed out that Traore was not charged with a hate crime and was confined to a mental institution, even though he showed no signs of mental illness. Some speculated that French authorities glossed over the uncomfortable facts of this case in order not to give ammunition to the

Presidential campaign of Marine Le Pen, who was calling for an end to France's open-door immigration policies.[201]

Reining in Marine Le Pen and the "far right" was more important to French authorities than reining in the likes of Kobili Traore.

The same denial prevailed in Britain. In June 2017, a Muslim was arrested after he wandered through Stamford Hill, a predominantly Jewish area of London screaming "Allah, Allah" and "I'm going to kill you all."[202] Like Kobili Traore, he was deemed mentally ill. A police spokesman explained: "He was detained by officers under the Mental Health Act. No one was injured. This is not being treated as terror-related."[203]

## Exporting jihad

As a result of mass Muslim migration into Europe, some European countries also became exporters of jihadis. One of the most notorious was the Islamic State's principal killer, the man whose knife sawed into the throats of many of the hostages that the terror group beheaded, including James Foley, Steven Sotloff, David Haines, Alan Henning, Peter Kassig, Haruna Yukawa, and Kenji Goto. While the Islamic State cameras rolled, he always wore a balaclava over his face and never announced who he was. Because he spoke with a pronounced English accent, he became known as "Jihadi John"—after John Lennon of the Beatles, with three other British Muslims in the Islamic State known as Paul, George, and Ringo.

"Jihadi John" turned out to be Mohammed Emwazi, a London resident in his mid-20s. Emwazi was born in Kuwait and moved with his family to London in 1994, where he lived a quiet middle-class existence and attended a Greenwich mosque. He graduated from the University of Westminster with a degree in computer programming.[204]

Once it became clear that Emwazi had not suffered from any of the poverty and alienation to which a Muslim's turn to jihad terror is usually attributed, the mainstream media began casting Emwazi as a victim of Britain's overzealous security services. Emwazi and two of his friends had flown to Tanzania in August 2009; they said they just wanted to go on safari, but authorities in Dar es Salaam refused him admission. In September 2009 he went to his native Kuwait; ten months later he returned to Britain and then was refused a visa to go back to Kuwait. "I had a job waiting for me and marriage to get started," Emwazi recounted. "I feel like a prisoner, only not in a cage, in London, a person imprisoned and controlled by security service men, stopping me from living my new life in my birthplace and country, Kuwait."[205]

This was the cause of Emwazi's "radicalization," said Asim Qureshi of Cage, a far-left group in Britain that agitates for the release of Guantanamo detainees and other jihadists. Qureshi complained, "When we treat people as if they are outsiders they will inevitably feel like outsiders—our entire national security strategy for the last 13 years has only increased alienation. A narrative of injustice has taken root."[206]

Perhaps—but does this "narrative of injustice" and alienation-producing national security strategy extend also to Tanzania? None of those who claimed that Emwazi had been "radicalized" by his supposedly unfair treatment at the hands of British security officials explained why it was not only the British who had denied Emwazi a visa to go to Kuwait, but also Tanzanian officials who had refused to let him into that country. Emwazi aroused the suspicion of security officials in not one but two nations long before he became "Jihadi John."

What's more, British authorities may have been so venomously "Islamophobic" that they spent their time and resources harassing innocent young Muslims like poor Mohammed Emwazi, but they were also so inattentive or overworked that they let Emwazi make his way to the Islamic State.

The Islamic State has not only attracted young Muslim men, but also hundreds of Muslim women from all over the world. British authorities estimated that 10% of the Muslims from Britain who have traveled to the Islamic State are women, and the same proportion of women went to the Islamic State from continental Europe, Australia, and the United States.[207] These girls went to the Islamic State to become the wives of jihad warriors; a small number of women have also taken up arms themselves.[208]

Some have made the trip while as young as 13, and many girls in their mid-teens have gone, including two Muslim teens from Vienna, Sabina Selimovic, 15, and Samra Kesinovic, 16. Before they left, Samra had become notorious around her school for speaking out for jihad and leaving graffiti around the building reading, "I love al-Qaeda." They left a note for their parents saying, "Don't look for us. We will serve Allah—and we will die for him."[209]

Not just die, but kill: before she left her home in Avignon, France for the Islamic State, Nora el-Bathy, 15, posted on Facebook a photo of a veiled woman holding a rifle, with the caption, "Yes, kill! In the name of Allah."[210]

Others betrayed just how young they really were. The twins Zahra and Salma Halane, 16, left England for the Islamic State, where Zahra posed for a photo in which she also was fully veiled, holding a rifle, and posing in front of the Islamic State's black flag of jihad. But on her social media account, she was soon after that lamenting the loss of her beloved kitten, who never returned home after her jihadist husband one night angrily threw it outside.[211]

Another reminder of these girls' extreme youth came in February 2015, when three Muslim schoolgirls from Britain—Amira Abase, 15; Shamima Begum, 15; and Khadiza Sultana, 16—sneaked away from their homes and families to join the Islamic State. Abase Hussen, the father of Amira Abase, appeared before the cameras clutching the girl's teddy bear and affecting shock, sorrow, and outrage that his daughter would do such a thing. He excoriated British authorities for failing to prevent the girls from leaving Britain. However, it later came to light that when she decided to make her trip to the caliphate, young Amira may have been acting upon teachings she had learned at home: in his pre-teddy bear clutching days, Abase Hussen had in 2012 attended a rally led by firebrand British jihad leader Anjem Choudhary, at which rallygoers chanted "Allahu akbar" and "The followers of Mohammed will conquer America."[212]

One 18-year-old Muslim woman from Britain, Umm Khattab, said that she would like to see "David Cameron's head on a spike" and fled the Sceptered Isle. Once safely in the caliphate, she took to Twitter to exhort other Muslim girls from Britain to join her. In Britain, she claimed fancifully, it was almost impossible to live in an Islamically correct manner: Muslims, she said, had been forced to sign a petition to head off the prohibition of halal meat (that is, meat from animals slaughtered according to the specifications of Islamic law).[213]

One of the Islamic State's female Sharia enforcers, Aqsa Mahmood, captured attention for her open praise of the murder of British soldier Lee Rigby on a London street in 2013, as well as for the Boston Marathon and Fort Hood jihad massacres. She saw these jihad attacks in the West as just as valuable as making the trip to the Islamic State: "If you cannot make it to the battlefield, then bring the battlefield to yourself."[214]

Aqsa Mahmood was the daughter of an immigrant from Pakistan who starred for Scotland's cricket team. She attended Craigholme, an upscale private school. Her parents noted that when the uprising against Assad began in Syria, Aqsa, who had been quite secular, became interested in her religion and began reading the Qur'an avidly. Ultimately, she fled from her home in Scotland to the Islamic State in November 2013, when she was 19.

Aqsa then took to social media to exhort other young Muslim girls to follow in her footsteps. She also confronted the idea that Muslims were drawn to jihad by poverty and social alienation:

> The media at first used to claim that the ones running away to join the Jihad as being unsuccessful, didn't have a future and from broke down families etc. But that is far from the truth. Most sisters I have come across have been in university studying courses with many promising paths, with big, happy families and friends and everything. If we had stayed behind, we could have been blessed with it all from a relaxing and comfortable life and lots of money.[215]

She said that Muslims who made their way to the Islamic State would receive "a house with free electricity and water provided to you due to the Khilafah and no rent included. Sounds great right?"[216] And as if that weren't enough, she wrote, they would receive "an even BIGGER reward in the Aakhirah (afterlife)."[217] She told potential journeyers to the Islamic State that certainly they would miss their families, but "the family you get in exchange for leaving the ones behind are like the pearl in comparison to the Shell you threw away into the foam of the sea."[218]

She emphasized that it was all about Islam: "To those who are able and can still make your way, hasten to our lands. . . . This is a war against Islam and it is known that either 'you're with them or with us'. So pick a side."[219] Aqsa warned, however, that girls who followed in her footsteps would baffle and grieve their more secular-minded parents:

> How does a parent who has little Islamic knowledge and understanding comprehend why their son or daughter has left their well-off life, education and a bright future behind to go live in a war-torn country. Most likely they will blame themselves, they will think they have done something. But until they truly understand from the bottom of their heart that you have done this action sincerely for Allah's sake they will live in hope that you will return.[220]

Aqsa emphasized that although she missed her own mother, she would not return to Britain. And she never did; Aqsa Mahmood is believed to have been killed in the ISIS domains.

# CHAPTER 5

## MIGRANTS AND EUROPEAN CULTURE

*Which culture had to adapt?*

Yet while the British media universally cast the problem in racial terms, the root cause was not racial at all, but ideological. Oussama Cherribi, a member of the Dutch Parliament, quoted an imam in Holland: "The *sharia* (Islamic law) does not have to adapt to the modern world because these are divine laws. People have to bend to the *sharia*."[221] Investigating the question of divorce, Cherribi interviewed 12 of the 15 imams in Amsterdam and found that 11 held "the most conservative position which give[s] women no rights in the matter of divorce"—in other words, Sharia.[222] And defense of Sharia includes defense of stoning. Hani Ramadan, a prominent Muslim leader in Switzerland, was dismissed from a teaching position in Geneva after publishing an article in the French journal *Le Monde* in September 2002 defending stoning as the punishment for adultery.[223]

According to the Roman Catholic Archbishop of Izmir, Turkey, Giuseppe Bernardini, in Europe "the 'dominion' has already begun." He noted that Saudi "petro-dollars" have been used "not to create work in the poor North African or Middle Eastern countries, but to build mosques and cultural centers in Christian countries with Islamic immigration, including Rome, the center of Christianity. . . . How can we ignore in all this a program of expansion and re-conquest?"

Bernardini recounted a conversation he had with a Muslim leader who said to him, "Thanks to your democratic laws, we will invade you. Thanks to our religious laws, we will dominate you."[224]

In December 2017, the British government issued a report known as the Casey Review (named for its author, Dame Louise Casey) that examined the fact, by then obvious to everyone, that many immigrant communities were not integrating. The report stated that "regressive religious and cultural ideologies" were in part responsible for this situation, along with native Britons who were reluctant to speak out about the state of affairs for fear of being "labelled racist."[225]

## A new Al-Andalus

The self-hatred of the European intelligentsia was in some cases so pronounced that recommendations that amounted essentially to cultural suicide could be warmly received and considered favorably in the highest circles.

Akbar Ahmed is an internationally respected and abundantly honored academic, holding the Ibn Khaldun chair of Islamic studies and holding a position as professor of international relations at the American University. He has also served as the Pakistani high commissioner to Britain and Ireland. He had entrée to the highest corridors of power and influence. He used this access to whitewash the historical record of Muslim Spain, not simply as a matter of correcting the historical record, but with a contemporary agenda: historical revisionism is frequently designed to influence current policy, and Ahmed's was no exception. Akbar Ahmed's whitewashes of Islamic Al-Andalus were clearly meant to break down resistance to the mass Muslim migrant influx into Europe today.

In his 2018 book *Journey into Europe*, Ahmed called for a "New Andalusia" in Europe. In a March 2018 article in Pakistan's *Daily Times*, he scolded, "Italy must remember its pluralist past."[226]

Ahmed assumed, as have so many others, that it was the responsibility of non-Muslims in the West, and no one else, to be "pluralist" and prove their "tolerance." Such analyses found a ready and eager audience among European leftists, who dominated the West's political culture. No one seemed to notice that there were never calls upon, for example, Saudi Arabia to remember its pluralist past, when Jews, Christians, and polytheists lived in Arabia. No one ever called upon Sharia states to be more tolerant of non-Muslims. The onus was always solely on the West.

Ahmed characterized the foes of mass Muslim migration in Italy as if they were all neo-Nazis, neo-fascists, and anti-Semites, with the strong implication that no one would have any reason for opposing that migration except for racism and xenophobia. He retailed, in highly misleading fashion, some historical incidents. Yet there is a great deal about Islam and Muslims in Italy that Akbar Ahmed didn't mention.

The Muslim conquest of Sicily began in 827. By 829, the jihadi invaders had been almost completely driven off the island when they received unexpected help: an invading Muslim army from Al-Andalus, led by Asbagh ibn Wakil. Although they ultimately took Palermo, the Muslims were not able to secure the eastern part of Sicily, stymied by both the ferocity of the native population and their own inability to unite their various factions. The fighting went on for decades.

In 878, the Muslims finally took Syracuse, and the booty was immense. According to the 18th-century historian Edward Gibbon, "the plate of the cathedral weighed five thousand pounds of silver; the entire spoil was computed at one million of pieces of gold [about 400,000 pounds sterling]."[227] Along with the treasure, the Muslims enslaved over 17,000 Christians. The exact number is not known, but according to Gibbon, it exceeded the number of the 17,000 Christians who were captured when the Muslims took Taormina and were sent to Africa to lead lives of slavery.

The warriors of jihad were finally able to secure complete control of Sicily in 902. The conquerors treated their new domains with extreme severity, brutally suppressing the Greek language and forcibly converting thousands of young boys to Islam.

Later, the Sicilians were able to drive the invaders out, but the devastation they had wrought was immense.

In another piece published in mid-June 2018, Ahmed claimed that the Islamic caliphate in Spain "more than any other came to represent the idea of pluralist society in Europe."[228]

In reality, Muslim Spain was anything but pluralist—it was miserable to live as a Christian there. Christians could never be sure that they would not be harassed. One contemporary account tells of priests being "pelted with rocks and dung" by Muslims while on the way to a cemetery.[229] The dhimmis suffered severe economic hardship: Paul Alvarus, a ninth-century Christian in Córdoba, complained about the "unbearable tax" that Muslims levied on Christians.[230] Nor could Christians say anything about their lot, because it was proscribed by Islamic law, and criticizing Islam, Muhammad, or the Qur'an in any manner was a death-penalty offense.

In 850, Perfectus, a Christian priest, engaged a group of Muslims in conversation about Islam; his opinion of the conquerors' religion was not positive. For this, Perfectus was arrested and put to death. Not long thereafter, Joannes, a Christian merchant, was said to have invoked Muhammad's name in his sales pitch. He was lashed and given a lengthy prison sentence. Christian and Muslim sources contain numerous records of similar incidents in the early part of the tenth century. Around 910, in one of many such episodes, a woman was executed for proclaiming that "Jesus was God and that Muhammad had lied to his followers."[231]

Far from being a paradise of tolerance, Umayyad Spain became a center of the Islamic slave trade. Muslim buyers could purchase sex-slave girls as young as 11 years old, as well as slave boys for sex, or slave boys raised to become slave soldiers. Also for sale were eunuchs, useful for guarding harems. Blonde slaves seized in jihad raids on Christian nations north of Al-Andalus were especially prized and fetched high prices. Slave traders would use makeup to whiten the faces and dye to lighten the hair of darker slaves so that they could get more money for them.

A 12th-century witness of the sale of sex slaves described the market:

> The merchant tells the slave girls to act in a coquettish manner with the old men and with the timid men among the potential buyers to make them crazy with desire. The merchant paints red the tips of the fingers of a white slave; he paints in gold those of a black slave; and he dresses them all in transparent clothes, the white female slaves in pink and the black ones in yellow and red.[232]

If the girls did not cooperate, of course, they would be beaten or killed.

The primary source of slaves was non-Muslims, as enslaving fellow Muslims was considered a violation of the Qur'an's requirement to be "merciful to one another" (48:29); hence, Muslim slave traders had to look to non-Muslim communities for merchandise.

Akbar Ahmed didn't mention any of that, because if the public knew those facts and others, they wouldn't favor the policies he wants the West to adopt. It interfered with his agenda, and that of the European elites, regarding migrants. Yet, as we have seen, when it comes to crime and sexual abuse, Akbar's "New Andalus" seems to have more in common with the grim historical reality of Muslim Spain than with his fanciful version.

## *Jahiliyya*

In March 2012, video surfaced of Muslims in Libya desecrating Australian war graves, just weeks after reports that Muslims there, in a rage over Qur'ans accidentally burned in Afghanistan, had also desecrated British graves.[233] Such behavior may have seemed puzzling to those who believed the statements of Muslim spokesmen in the West about how Islam tolerated and respected non-believers and non-Muslim religions; in fact, however, such behavior was fully in accord with standard Islamic theology regarding the nature of non-believing society and the value of its cultural artifacts. The implications of this for mass Muslim migration into Europe were as obvious as they were ominous.

The general Islamic term for the period of history before the advent of Islam, as well as the pre-Islamic period of any nation's history, is *jahiliyya*, or the period of ignorance and barbarism. Consequently, any art, literature, or architecture that any non-Islamic culture produces has no value whatsoever: it is all simply a manifestation of that ignorance and barbarism. The celebrated writer V. S. Naipaul encountered this attitude in his travels through the Islamic world. For Muslims, he observed, "The time before Islam is a time of blackness: that is part of Muslim theology. History has to serve theology."[234]

Naipaul explained how some Pakistani Muslims, far from valuing the nation's renowned archaeological site at Mohenjo Daro, see it as a teaching opportunity for Islam:

> A featured letter in *Dawn* offered its own ideas for the site. Verses from the Koran, the writer said, should be engraved and set up in Mohenjo-Daro in "appropriate places": "Say (unto them, O Mohammed): Travel in the land and see the nature of the sequel for the guilty. . . . Say (O Mohammed, to the disbelievers): Travel in the land and see the nature of the consequence for those who were before you. Most of them were idolaters."[235]

In other words, Mohenjo Daro has no value for what it reveals about an ancient civilization. Its value is solely in its present condition as a ruin, a sign for the unbelievers of Allah's wrath. Likewise in Iran. Naipaul notes, "In 637 A.D., just five years after the death of the Prophet, the Arabs began to overrun Persia, and all Persia's great past, the past before Islam, was declared a time of blackness."[236]

The Christians of Europe could suffer the same fate. In March 2013, the Egyptian Islamic scholar Abdullah Badr demonstrated how such beliefs about the society of unbelievers being a time of blackness, and thus the people who created that civilization being contemptible, can work out in practice. He explained that Christians disgusted him, saying that it was "not a matter of piety, but disgust. I get grossed out. Get that? Disgust, I get grossed out, man, I cannot stand their smell or . . . I don't like them, it's my choice. And they gross me out; their smell, their look, everything. I feel disgusted, disgusted."[237]

That disgust has combined with imperatives derived from Qur'anic injunctions to "slay the polytheists wherever you find them" (9:5) and to subjugate the People of the Book (9:29) to play out in Islamic history in the cleansing of entire regions of their non-Muslim populations. Eliminating other religions, as per Qur'an 8:39 ("fight . . . until religion is all for Allah") and making sure that any non-Muslims who remain are conquered and submissive is the overarching goal of *jihad*. As an Iranian Bahai observed to V. S. Naipaul in the course of his travels through the world of Islam, "These Muslims are a strange people. They have an *old* mentality. Very *old* mentality. They are very bad to minorities."[238]

The transformation of Constantinople following its conquest in 1453 illustrates the effects of Muslim bigotry. Before the Muslim conquest, Constantinople had been the center of Eastern Christianity and the second city of all Christendom, as well as the chief rival to the splendor and authority of Rome. Its Hagia Sophia cathedral, built by the Emperor Justinian in the sixth century, was the grandest and most celebrated church in the Christian world until the construction of St. Peter's in the Vatican. As recently as 1914, Constantinople still boasted a population nearly 50% Christian. Today, as a result of the religious persecution of Christians, the city is now 99.99% Muslim.[239]

After the 1453 Muslim conquest, the Hagia Sophia Cathedral, like so many other Christian churches before and after, was transformed into a mosque. After Turkey's secularization, the mosque was converted into a museum by the secularists and is now about to be transformed into a mosque again. While secular Turkey did not enforce Islamic law, it saw a depoliticized Islam as essential to the Turkish identity—at the expense of the Christian population. In Tur-Abdin in southwest Turkey in 1960, there were 150,000 Christians; today there are just over 2,000.[240] The rest have fled in the face of Muslim hostility and harassment.

In Turkey itself, the Christian population has declined from 15% in 1920 to 1% today. In Syria, the Christian population has declined from 33% to 10% in the same span. Since the Turks occupied northern Cyprus in 1974, churches have been despoiled of their icons, which have flooded the market in Greece. The Turks have taken over many churches for secular uses and even tried to convert the fourth-century Christian monastery of San Makar into a hotel. Christian Cypriots are forbidden to come near the building, much less enter it.[241]

Likewise in Tunisia, "in the early 1950s, half of the inhabitants of Tunis were Catholics, but with the declaration of independence some 280,000

Tunisian Catholics were expelled. Today there are no more than a tenth of this number and most of the churches are closed or no longer in use."[242]

The non-Muslim graves in Libya were not, of course, central elements of any country's cultural patrimony. But the Muslims who felt free to desecrate them were working from the same attitude of contempt for unbelievers and their works. "Muhammad is the Messenger of God," says the Qur'an, "and those who are with him are hard against the unbelievers, merciful one to another" (48:29). While Muslims are "the best nation ever brought forth to men" (3:110), the "unbelievers of the People of the Book" (that is, Jews and Christians who have refused to become Muslim) "and the idolaters" are the "worst of creatures" (98:6).

When the "worst of creatures" do something that the "best nation ever brought forth to men" finds offensive, the "worst of creatures" have no rights that the members of the "best nation" are bound to respect. This holds true even of the dead, who died in unbelief and are thus being tortured in hell by Allah: "We shall certainly roast them at a Fire; as often as their skins are wholly burned, We shall give them in exchange other skins, that they may taste the chastisement. Surely God is All-mighty, All-wise" (4:56).

Ultimately, the "worst of creatures" must submit to the rule and hegemony of the "best nation." The 20th-century Muslim Brotherhood theorist Sayyid Qutb declared,

> If we look at the sources and foundations of modern ways of living, it becomes clear that the whole world is steeped in *Jahiliyyah*, and all the marvelous material comforts and high-level inventions do not diminish this ignorance. This *Jahiliyyah* is based on rebellion against God's sovereignty on earth. It transfers to man one of the greatest attributes of God, namely sovereignty, and makes some men lords over others.[243]

The way to restore Allah's sovereignty over the earth is to impose Islamic law (Sharia), which mandates a subjugated second-class status for non-Muslims.

It was in this context that the graves were desecrated. Islam mandates a sharp dichotomy between believers and unbelievers, who in the Islamic vision of society can only live in harmony with one another when non-Muslims know their place and submit to the Muslims. The desecration of the graves in Libya was a direct consequence of non-Muslims not knowing that place and not submitting.

As such, non-Muslim analysts would do well not to see these desecrations as isolated incidents. But given that willful blindness about the ways in which jihadists use the texts and teachings of Islam to justify violence and supremacism is now official dogma in Washington, never to be questioned, it is much more likely that these incidents will be brushed aside or ignored altogether in the continued quixotic and ever-fruitless effort by the leaders of the "worst of creatures" to win hearts and minds among those of the "best of nations."

One manifestation of those efforts to win hearts and minds was the wholesale cultural capitulation of many areas of Britain and continental Europe.

## Britain's capitulation

In this atmosphere of cultural capitulation, it was no surprise that many of the cultural accommodations Britain made for its new and rapidly growing Muslim population bordered on the risible:

- British schools dropped teaching about the Holocaust for fear that Muslim students would find the lessons offensive.[244]
- British officials spent thousands of pounds reorienting prison toilets so that they wouldn't face Mecca (Islam forbids Muslims to face Mecca or turn their back to it when urinating or defecating).[245]
- The Association of Chief Police Officers ordered that police sniffer dogs wear "booties" when searching inside the homes of Muslim suspects, in order to avoid offending against the Islamic principle that dogs are unclean.[246]
- The British banks Halifax and NatWest banned piggy banks to keep from offending Muslims, as Islam also considers pigs unclean. Despite the fact that piggy banks do not include any pork or pork products, Salim Mulla of the Lancashire Council of Mosques, was pleased: "This is a sensitive issue and I think the banks are simply being courteous to their customers."[247]
- A non-Muslim teacher disciplined two schoolchildren after they refused to participate in classroom exercises that involved reciting Islamic prayers. The mother of one of the boys commented: "This isn't right, it's taking things too far. I understand that they have to learn about other religions. I can live with that but it is taking it a

step too far to be punished because they wouldn't join in Muslim prayer. Making them pray to Allah, who isn't who they worship, is wrong and what got me is that they were told they were being disrespectful." Another parent remarked, "The school is wonderful but this one teacher has made a major mistake. It seems to be happening throughout society. People think they can ride roughshod over our beliefs and the way we live."[248]

- An 18-year-old boy with Down's syndrome and a mental age of five was charged with "racial assault" after a playground scuffle with a Muslim schoolmate at the special needs department of Motherwell College in Lanarkshire.[249]

The inevitable outcome of this appeasement policy came in August 2008, when Muslim town council leaders at the Tower Hamlets Council in east London issued edicts banning all councilors, Muslim and non-Muslim, from eating during meetings before sunset during Ramadan. One non-Muslim councilor, Stephanie Eaton, protested: "Our community consists of a huge number of different religions, all of which should be valued, and no one religion should be accorded more status or influence than others."[250]

She was, of course, right about that, but she and all British non-Muslims should have known that the Tower Hamlets Council food ban was an inevitable result of the accommodation of Muslim practices in Britain. And more would come.

## The call to prayer on the BBC

Global Village Space reported in April 2020 that "in a first, BBC begins the broadcast of Muslim prayers on its network as mosques shut down across Britain, part of the extensive measures against coronavirus."[251] In today's Britain, it is extraordinarily unlikely that the BBC will stop broadcasting the *adhan*, the Islamic call to prayer, once the coronavirus pandemic is over. A cultural line has been crossed. And the implications of this, beyond the expected hosannas from the usual proponents of globalism and multiculturalism, are ominous.

According to Global Village Space,

different imams lead the 5:50 am broadcasts every week on Friday from 14 local radio stations of BBC. The imam recites verses from the Holy Quran and quotes of Holy Prophet before delivering the sermon and leading the listeners in prayers. The program is titled, 'Islamic Reflections'. The arrangements have been made to facilitate the Muslim community to the run-up to the month of Ramadan till the end of April.[252]

The BBC was no doubt thrilled to do this, as it demonstrated how "inclusive" the mega-network was, and how welcoming British society was. Chris Burns, the head of BBC Local Radio, was pleased, saying, "Local radio is all about connecting communities, and we hope these weekly reflections will go some way to helping Muslims feel a sense of community while they are isolating."[253]

BBC CWR presenter Phil Upton added,

> Ramadan is just a few weeks away and I appreciate that for many that's a big void to fill with as many as one and a half hours of your day, especially in the evening, in Ramadan month, spent in your local mosque. With many local mosques being closed because of the coronavirus outbreak there's an overwhelming sadness with the loss of your spiritual connection that can be gained from congregational prayers, so we are trying to fill the void in some small way with Islamic reflections.[254]

The adhan, prayed in Arabic, repeats "Allahu akbar" six times, "I testify that there is no god but Allah" three times, and "I testify that Muhammad is Allah's prophet" twice.

Dr. Gavin Ashenden, former Chaplain to the British Queen, who resigned his position in protest against a Qur'an reading in a Scottish church, observed that "the Muslim call to prayer is a dramatic piece of Islamic triumphalism. It proclaims Islam's superiority over all other religions, and in so doing casts Jesus in the role of a charlatan and a liar. The Muslim god, Allah, is unknowable and has no son. Jesus was, therefore, a fraud in claiming He and the Father are one."[255]

Was the BBC, the government-funded broadcasting agency of an ostensibly Christian land, really wise to broadcast a declaration of the superiority of another faith, one that directs its adherents to make war against Christians and subjugate them as inferiors under the hegemony of believers (cf. Qur'an 9:29)?

Was the BBC wise to broadcast the cry "Allahu akbar," beloved of jihad terrorists the world over? Chief 9/11 hijacker Mohammed Atta wrote this in his letter to himself before carrying out his jihad mission: "When the confrontation begins, strike like champions who do not want to go back to this world. Shout, 'Allahu Akbar,' because this strikes fear in the hearts of the non-believers."[256] This is why the Fort Hood jihad killer, Nidal Malik Hasan, shouted it as he shot 13 Americans in November 2009, and why so many other jihadis have used it essentially as an announcement that non-Muslims are about to die.

## Inclusivity

The BBC would no doubt defend its decision to broadcast the adhan on the grounds of inclusivity. That had been the pretext for cultural abdication for quite some time. In December 2019, according to the Mail on Sunday, "children at a primary school have been told not to sing the word 'Lord' in the Christmas carol Away In A Manger—so that pupils of all beliefs can join in. . . . Youngsters at Whitehall Primary School in Chingford, Essex, have also been told to sing edited versions of two modern hymns when they attend a carol service and nativity play at a nearby church on Tuesday. The words 'Jesus the saviour' in the carol Love Shone Down have been replaced with 'Jesus the baby', while the words 'new King born today' in the carol Come And Join The Celebration have been replaced with 'a baby born today.'"[257]

Whitehall Primary School Head Teacher Zakia Khatun explained that she didn't want students of other beliefs to feel "excluded."[258] She "defended her decision, insisting the school is inclusive of all children, and maintained that last year 60 children did not attend the carol service and nativity at St Peter and St Paul Church in Chingford because of their religious beliefs."[259]

Britain has been home to non-Christians for centuries, and they never complained about Christmas carols. There was only one group in Britain that might object to calling Jesus "Lord," and that group isn't likely to attend the Christmas pageant now that the word has been removed, because the whole idea of celebrating the birth of Jesus is predicated upon the now-unmentionable title.

One mother noted, "If he was just a baby boy named Jesus, there wouldn't be a celebration in the first place. He is our Lord and Saviour and King of all Kings—that's the whole point. It is also a tradition—it is taking away the traditions of the country."[260] Indeed.

## Sharia speech restrictions

The censorious approach of the British authorities, which they adopted to avoid offending Muslim believers, extends far beyond Christmas hymns.

The *Daily Mail* reported in June 2017 that "police have arrested two people on suspicion of racial hatred after a video appeared online showing a man burning a copy of the Koran."[261]

The arrests of these Qur'an-burners were an attempt at shoring up the sagging narrative in Britain of a "far-right" threat and buttressing the claim that this racist, xenophobic "far right" constituted just as much of a threat to Britons as Islamic jihadis.

Ironically, just three days later, Sky News reported that in a raid of a safe house that the jihadis who murdered 11 people and wounded 48 in an attack on the London Bridge on June 3, 2017, had used, "investigators found an English-language copy of the Koran opened at a page describing martyrdom."[262]

The arrests of the Qur'an-burners showed that in response to the London Bridge massacre, British Prime Minister Theresa May and the British political establishment started their nation down the path of Sharia compliance by arresting people for violating Sharia blasphemy law regarding the disposal of the Qur'an. It was not, in reality, an act of "racial hatred" to burn a Qur'an. The Qur'an is not a race, and neither is Islam; there are Muslims of all races. These arrests were just another example of the British government's exaggerated solicitude for Muslims, which stemmed from the false assumption that jihad violence is the result of the "marginalization" of Muslim communities.

The May government was staking the future of Britain on the idea that being nice to Muslims, and moving swiftly and strongly against violations of Sharia blasphemy laws such as the burning of Qur'ans, would end the jihad against Britain. They would be proven mistaken in this again and again.

Also, May's government took no notice at all of what the burned Qur'ans really signified: the frustration and anger of an increasing number of Britons at the political establishment's supine response to the jihad threat. I am not in favor of burning books myself and would prefer people read and understand what is in the Qur'an rather than burn it, but no one can miss the source of the burners' frustration. And with these arrests, that frustration was only going to get worse.

The Sharia supremacism that the British establishment not only tolerated but encouraged would ultimately turn its full force upon its benefactors.

## Britain's Sharia courts

That day was being hastened in Britain's Sharia courts. Many Muslims spoke publicly, or in forums where the text or video of what they said was readily available, about their intention to impose Islamic Sharia law upon the non-Muslim populations of Western countries as soon as possible. They are doing so today by portraying accommodation of Islamic law as a matter of "civil rights" and multiculturalist "diversity."

In response, British authorities did all they could to give them what they wanted. The effort to bring Sharia to Britain got a tremendous shot in the arm in July 2008, when the Lord Chief Justice, Lord Phillips of Worth Matravers, said in an address at the London Muslim Centre that "it is possible in this country for those who are entering into a contractual agreement to agree that the agreement shall be governed by law other than English law."[263] Including Islamic law? Yes: "There is no reason why principles of sharia, or any other religious code, should not be the basis for mediation or other forms of alternative dispute resolution. "[264]

At first glance, there was nothing remarkable in this. The Lord Chief Justice was calling simply for the voluntary application of Sharia in private arbitration and emphasized that the decisions of such arbitration would be subject to British law: "So far as the law is concerned," he explained, "those who live in this country are governed by English and Welsh law and subject to the jurisdiction of the English and Welsh courts."[265] As such, "it must be recognised however that any sanctions for a failure to comply with the agreed terms of the mediation would be drawn from the laws of England and Wales."[266]

What's more, he decisively rejected the idea that the notorious Sharia penalties of stoning for adultery and amputation for theft would be implemented in Britain: "There can be no question of such sanctions being applied to or by any Muslim who lives within this jurisdiction."[267]

But if he hedged his statement about the use of Sharia for private arbitration so carefully, why were the Lord Chief Justice's remarks a victory for the stealth jihad endeavor to establish the hegemony of Sharia in Britain? The answer to this lies in the nature of Sharia itself. In Islamic law, private matters are not so easy to separate from public ones. If a woman is judged in a private Sharia court to be guilty of adultery, the Sharia penalty is stoning. The Lord Chief Justice spoke coolly of not allowing such punishments, but once the principle that Sharia can be applied in Britain is accepted, calls to increase its scope will begin immediately. The next step will be challenges to the principle he stated that whenever British law and Sharia come into conflict, Sharia must give way. And given the prevailing multiculturalist relativism, soon enough that principle will give way also.

In his address, Lord Phillips praised the Archbishop of Canterbury, Rowan Williams, who famously said in February 2008 that it was "inevitable" that Sharia would come to Britain. "An approach to law which simply said— there's one law for everybody—I think that's a bit of a danger," said the Archbishop.[268] He had apparently forgotten, if he ever knew, that the idea of "one law for everybody" was one of the great achievements of Judeo-Christian civilization and was rooted in the idea of the dignity of all human beings as created in the image of God. Once a society discards the principle of "one law for everybody," it has laid the groundwork for protected and privileged classes and inevitably ends up with a tyranny in which some groups are denied basic rights.

The first of these to suffer this denial from Sharia courts were Muslim women. In March 2015, The Bow Group, a British think tank, issued a report noting that as a result of the Sharia courts, Muslim women in Britain were not receiving justice in cases of domestic violence and were suffering the inequalities mandated for women in divorces and inheritance rights, as well as the dehumanization of polygamy. One Muslim woman lamented, "I feel betrayed by Britain. I came here to get away from this and the situation is worse here than in the country I escaped from."[269] The Sharia courts often prevented Muslim women from seeking aid from outside their communities by warning them that to do so would bring "shame" and "dishonor" to them and their families.[270]

British Prime Minister Theresa May promised a review of the Sharia courts and their respect for British law, but the UK's *Independent* reported in July 2016 that May's review had been

> branded a 'whitewash' before it has even begun, with more than 200 individuals and human rights groups signing an open letter urging her to dismantle the panel chosen to oversee the inquiry. They claim that by appointing an Islamic scholar as chair and placing two imams in advisory roles, the panel's ability to make an impartial assessment

of how religious arbitration is used to the detriment of women's rights will be seriously compromised.[271]

As expected, nothing came of May's review, and the worst fears of critics of the Sharia courts proved to be well founded. The UK's *Express* revealed in November 2016 that

> Sharia courts are sentencing women to lives of misery by ordering them to stay with abusive husbands, a rape victim has claimed. The mother-of-two, calling herself Lubna, revealed that she had been beaten, robbed and raped by her estranged husband despite the British courts banning him from approaching her and which had also awarded her custody of their children. But family pressure persuaded the British-Pakistani to try and obtain an Islamic divorce in a Sharia court.[272]

Lubna had hoped to find a sympathetic ear from the court, but the Sharia judges instead told her that she had to return to her husband, as abusive as he was. According to human rights activist Gita Sahgal of One Law for All, a group dedicated to working against the Sharia courts, Lubna's experience was not unique. Sahgal noted that the courts judged strictly by Islamic, rather than British, norms: "Any woman who embarks on a new relationship will, they say, have committed adultery—a crime only equalled in their eyes by apostasy, abandoning Islam, and blasphemy."[273] This was, she said, even stricter in its application of Sharia than courts in some majority-Muslim countries: "Yet the courts in, for example, Bangladesh and Pakistan, are perfectly happy to accept a civil divorce certificate from Britain as evidence of the end of a marriage, which in the Muslim tradition is a civil contract rather than a sacrament. In those countries, the contract must be registered to count as a legal marriage."[274]

The head of the UK Board of Sharia Councils, Dr. Ahmad al-Dubayan, noted that "everywhere in the country" there were Sharia courts in operation that were ignoring British law and the regulations that had been devised to govern such courts.[275] Al-Dubayan said that even the number of Sharia courts operating in Britain was unknown to British authorities: "We don't know how many councils there are. Some people talk about 80 or 30 or 50, I don't know. There is no record for this and no studies, unfortunately."

Naz Shah, a Labour MP and a Muslim herself, stated that the Sharia courts could "oppress" women and declared, "You cannot enforce and have a second parallel legal system in this country. As a British lawmaker I'm very clear, we have one law and that law is of the British court."[276]

In March 2017, a documentary revealed that the number of unsupervised Sharia courts had continued to grow. At that point, there were 85, and that number has only grown since then. The documentary showed one of the court proceedings as a woman pleaded with the Sharia courts to be allowed to divorce her emotionally abusive drug-dealer husband. The judges granted her the divorce, but the entire proceeding only emphasized the inequality of the sexes mandated by Sharia, for while women had to go to Sharia courts to request a divorce, all a man had to do in order to get a divorce was tell his wife, "I divorce you."[277]

Despite such reports, however, the number of Sharia courts in Britain continued to grow, with no increase in government supervision.

## Silencing critics in France

French authorities have also been reluctant to antagonize their growing and restive Muslim minority. The multiculturalism that has utterly taken over among the Western intelligentsia has made it difficult for them to take action against Muslim jihadist doctrines, even when they threaten the stability of secular society. According to Michel Zaoui of the Representative Council of Jewish Institutions in France (CRIF), "The previous leftist government didn't do anything to discourage anti-Israel and anti-Semitic propositions by militant Islamic preachers, in part because their philosophy was to show sympathy to the 'damned' and poor. Now, the rightist government would like to act but is afraid of antagonizing Muslims."[278]

Indeed, when the popular French writer Michel Houellebecq called Islam "the stupidest religion" and "a dangerous religion right from the start," he was hauled into court on charges of inciting racial hatred—though, of course, Muslims are of all races. The rector of the Grand Mosque of Paris, Dalil Boubakeur, who is generally regarded as supportive of the French secular regime, cried, "Islam has been reviled, attacked with hateful words. My community has been humiliated."

Houellebecq faced a €70,000 fine and 18 months in prison, but he was ultimately cleared of the charges. The late Italian journalist Oriana Fallaci, author of a rhetorical attack on Islam entitled *The Rage and the Pride*, faced unsuccessful attempts by French Muslims to get the book banned.[279] The guardians of "tolerable" speech had better luck against '60s screen siren

Brigitte Bardot, who has been convicted five times in her native France for "inciting racial hatred"—in every case for remarks considered denigrating to Muslims. In June 2008, a court fined the 73-year-old Bardot €15,000 (around $23,000) as a punishment for writing that the Islamic community in France was "destroying our country and imposing its acts."[280] The court apparently didn't consider the possibility that imposing Islamic law was precisely what many Muslims in France had in mind.

Though the charges against Houllebecq and Fallaci didn't stick, these trials set a dangerous precedent. While one can say anything one desires about Christianity without facing criminal charges, Islam is regarded as a protected minority religion—and perhaps, covertly, as being too volatile to criticize without risk of violence.

Meanwhile, Islam is on the march in France, as has been seen with the electoral success early in the decade of the Union of French Islamic Organizations (UOIF), which represents most of the 1,500 mosques in France. The UOIF is linked to both the Saudi Wahhabis and the Egyptian Muslim Brotherhood.[281] At the beginning of the Iraq war in 2003, the Brotherhood recruited several thousand Egyptians to fight in Iraq in the name of jihad.[282] In France, the UOIF is a voice of Islamic reaction—at its conventions (which have been attended by upwards of 100,000 people), it sponsors workshops with titles such as "Liberated Women, De-Natured Women."[283] UOIF Secretary-General Fouad Alaoui, after negotiations with the government on the status of Muslims in France, announced that he rejected a "definition of secularism that seals off religion in the private sphere." UOIF President Thami Breze declared his support for a "modification of secularism, in order to respect certain specificities of Islam."[284] Just as Czechoslovakia's borders had to be modified in 1938 to appease Hitler, so would French secularism have to be modified in the 21st century to appease the social and political imperatives of Muslims in France.

In the face of this, the French government created an Islamic Council that would ease the integration of Muslims into French society as a whole. This initially backfired, when in April 2003, the UOIF won 19 of 58 seats on the Council, compared to only 15 for the group favored by the government, the moderate Mosque of Paris.[285] Also, some 20% of French mosques refused to have anything at all to do with the Council, which was formed with the express purpose of creating an "official Islam for France."[286]

Why would the French government want to create an "official Islam for France"? Perhaps it is because the French government recognizes Islam as a looming threat to France's identity and sovereignty. Journalist Christopher Caldwell noted in 2003 that "practically all of France's 1,200 mosques are funded by foreign governments. Of the country's 230 major imams, none is French. In fact, imams are often chosen by foreign governments for loyalty to their ideological priorities. These priorities are decidedly not those of France. One imam in Roubaix met Lille mayor Martine Aubry on the edge of the Muslim-majority neighborhood where he preaches, declaring it Islamic territory into which Mme. Aubry—the most important minister of labor in modern French history, the early favorite to win France's presidential elections in 2007, and the daughter of former Prime Minister Jacques Delors—had no authority to venture."[287]

And according to Antoine Sfeir of Paris's Middle East Studies Center, "For a long time the UOIF has been trying to infiltrate the cogs of state and assume control of the Muslim community by marginalising secular Muslims."[288]

Mme. Aubry, of course, was not elected President of France in 2007. Nicolas Sarkozy was—a man who had appeared to be anything but an appeaser after the UOIF's electoral victory, when he was Interior Minister. At that time, Sarkozy warned Islamic extremists, "We want to say very simply: imams who propagate views that run counter to French values will be expelled."[289] This largely proved to be an empty threat. At the same time as he issued it, Sarkozy also affirmed that Muslims had a place in France: "It is precisely because we recognize the right of Islam to sit at the table of the republic that we will not accept any deviation. . . . Any prayer leader whose views run contrary to the values of the republic will be expelled."[290] And Sharia? "Islamic law will not apply anywhere, because it is not the law of the French republic."[291]

Despite these strong words, Sharia continued to advance in France. By 2020, Sarkozy was long gone, but French President Emmanuel Macron said much the same things as his antecedent had so many years before. In a speech on February 18, 2020, Macron declared,

> We must never accept that the laws of religion can be superior to those of the Republic. . . . Islamist separatism is incompatible with freedom and equality. . . . We are talking about people who, in the name of a religion, are pursuing a political project, that of a political Islam that wants to secede from our Republic. . . . In the Republic . . . we cannot accept that we refuse to shake hands with a woman because she is a woman. In the Republic, we cannot accept that someone refuses to be treated or educated by someone because she

is a woman. In the Republic, one cannot accept school dropouts for religious or belief reasons. In the Republic, one cannot require certificates of virginity to marry.[292]

Macron's words might have had more force if they hadn't simply been rehashes of vows made by his predecessors many years before. As far back as March 2007, shortly before he was elected President, Sarkozy affirmed French cultural integrity when asked about Islamic polygamy, which was widely practiced in France:

Question: What do you think of polygamy?

> Answer: I respect all cultures throughout the world, but so that it is quite clear: if I am elected President of the Republic, I will not accept women being treated as inferior to men. The French Republic holds these values: respect for women, equality between men and women. Nobody has the right to hold a prisoner, even within his own family. I say it clearly, that polygamy is prohibited in the territory of the French Republic. I will fight against female genital mutilation and those who do not wish to understand that the values of the French Republic include freedom for women, the dignity of women, respect for women—they do not have any reason to be in France. If our laws are not respected and if one does not wish to understand our values, if one does not wish to learn French, then one does not have any reason to be on French territory.[293]

For statements of this kind, Sarkozy was widely vilified among Muslims in France, to the extent that when he was elected President, young Muslim men in Paris rioted, smashing store windows and fighting with police in protest against his victory.[294] Yet for all his fearsome reputation, Sarkozy also favored policies that opened the door to the appeasement of Muslims in France, and ultimately to the advancement of an Islamic supremacist agenda that would, in accordance with traditional Islamic law, relegate non-Muslims and women to inferior status. By the time of Macron's statements, that door to appeasement had been open for years.

Sarkozy was one of those who had opened it. In the wake of the November 2005 Islamic riots that convulsed the country, Sarkozy, then Interior Minister, spoke out in favor of "positive discrimination" that would give preferential treatment to Muslims applying for jobs.[295]

## *Silencing critics in the Netherlands*

And in March 2008, when Dutch politician Geert Wilders issued his film *Fitna*, which was critical of the way in which Muslims have used the Qur'an to justify violent acts, Sarkozy sided with Dutch Prime Minister Jan Peter Balkenende, who criticized Wilders. After Balkenende stated that he was in "total disagreement" with Wilders and warned that the film could lead to violent Muslim protests, Sarkozy said that he supported Balkenende, and, according to a spokesman, was "highly aware of the question of Islam's place in European societies, and French society in particular."[296] Balkenende also tried to mollify Muslims by publicly disavowing the connection between Islam and violence: "We reject this interpretation," he declared. "The vast majority of Muslims reject extremism and violence."[297] That may have been so, but it did nothing to deter or forestall the plans of those Muslims who readily associated Islam with violence.

In reality, the film *Fitna* was simply accurate in depicting how Islamic jihadists justified their actions by reference to the Qur'an. Balkenende, Sarkozy, and other European heads of state should have defended it. It was extremely unfortunate that they did not, and did not even seem to understand the full dimensions of the problem. For the release of the film became the pretext for an energetic effort by international Islamic organizations to restrict free speech in the West, particularly regarding Islam. At a time when Muslims around the world are committing acts of violence and justifying them by reference to Islamic teachings, this would restrict Western officials and media analysts from discussing the Islamic supremacist threat precisely at the moment when they were directly confronted by it.

The demand for legal protection from criticism remained a central focus of the world's most powerful Islamic organization, the Organization of the Islamic Conference (OIC), which is composed of 57 governments of Muslim-majority states (including the reified "State of Palestine"). The OIC in 2008 declared its intention to craft a "legal instrument" to fight against the threat to Islam they perceived "from political cartoonists and bigots."[298] "Islamophobia," declared OIC Secretary General Ekmeleddin Ihsanoglu, "cannot be dealt with only through cultural activities but (through) a robust political engagement." This is a careful euphemism calling for restrictions on freedom of speech. Abdoulaye Wade, the President of Senegal and chairman of the OIC, made this point explicit: "I don't think freedom of expression should mean freedom from blasphemy. There can be no freedom without limits."[299]

The OIC stepped up its international campaign against free speech when *Fitna* appeared. The organization condemned the film in "the strongest terms," claiming that Wilders' movie was "a deliberate act of discrimination against Muslims" intended only to "provoke unrest and intolerance."[300]

By June 2008, Ihsanoglu was ready to declare victory in clearly supremacist terms: Muslims had dictated to the West the "red lines that should not be crossed," and the West was complying. He said that OIC initiatives against "Islamophobia" had resulted in "convincing progress at all these levels mainly the UN Human Rights Council in Geneva, and the UN General Assembly. The United Nations General Assembly adopted similar resolutions against the defamation of Islam." He added,

> In confronting the Danish cartoons and the Dutch film "Fitna", we sent a clear message to the West regarding the red lines that should not be crossed. As we speak, the official West and its public opinion are all now well-aware of the sensitivities of these issues. They have also started to look seriously into the question of freedom of expression from the perspective of its inherent responsibility, which should not be overlooked.[301]

The success of this campaign boded ill for the ability of those states to defend themselves against the global jihad in all its forms—since Islamic supremacists and their allies routinely characterized all investigation of the Islamic roots of the jihadist agenda as "hate speech." Sarkozy's unwillingness or inability to see what was at stake—a malady he shared with virtually all European leaders of his day and of the present time as well—boded ill for Europe's future as a home of free people.

## "Assimilation is cultural rape"

These attitudes, now deeply ingrained, were a long time in the making. The Arab European League (AEL), a Muslim advocacy organization in Belgium and the Netherlands, provides an illustrative example of what took place on practically a continent-wide scale. Founded by a Lebanese Muslim immigrant named Dyab Abou Jahjah, whom the *New York Times* dubbed "Belgium's Malcolm X," the AEL reassured many when it went on record saying that it opposed the imposition of Sharia in Holland.[302] With magnificent contempt, Jahjah said, "We're not folkloristic clowns who want to force Islamic law on other people."[303] The AEL stated that as part of its "vision and philosophy . . . We believe in a multicultural society as a social and political model where different cultures coexist with equal rights under the law."

The League operated as an advocacy group for Muslims against the backdrop of increasing tensions between Muslims and non-Muslims in Europe. Jahjah claimed that conditions for European Muslims have gotten even worse since September 11: "11 September also meant a new era for many Arabs and Muslims living abroad. It meant that the anti-Islamic sentiment which is inherent in European culture, but that had been marginalised by the politically-correct mainstream, could now manifest itself again."[304]

The AEL positioned itself as the defender of these Muslims. "Only strong communities are treated as equal," it asserted. "Therefore we must work within the boundaries of the law towards eliminating social-economic problems and creating the necessary organisational structures and tools in order to achieve a more dignified and empowered position as a community."

Yet more disquieting was the AEL's proclamation that Muslims in Europe "do not want to assimilate."[305] It continued: "We want to foster our own identity and culture while being law abiding and worthy citizens of the countries where we live. In order to achieve that it is imperative for us to teach our children the Arabic language and history and the Islamic faith. We will resist any attempt to strip us of our right to our own cultural and religious identity, as we believe it is one of the most fundamental human rights."[306] Jahjah declared: "Assimilation is cultural rape. It means renouncing your identity, becoming like the others."[307]

When Jahjah arrived in Belgium in 1991, he identified himself as a member of the Shi'ite terrorist group Hezbollah. He explained his desire to enter Belgium as part of his flight from the Hezbollah leadership after a dispute, although he later denied having been a member of Hezbollah: "That was a lie. I was a 19-year-old boy and I had to make up a story so I could get asylum. I emigrated because I wanted a better life."[308]

Maybe it was a lie. Nonetheless, when Jahjah was arrested in November 2002 and charged with inciting Muslims in Antwerp to riot, his rhetoric sounded much like that of Hezbollah (which refers to Israel as the "Zionist enemy"). He charged that "he was being demonized by manipulators in the Belgian government and the 'Zionist lobby.'"[309] Belgian Prime Minister Guy

Verhofstadt declared that the Arab European League was "trying to terrorize the city."[310] Navma Elmaslouhi, press officer for AEL's new branch in Holland, "was quoted as telling Saturday's Handelsblad newspaper . . . that she didn't disapprove of Moroccan youngsters chanting 'Hamas, Hamas, gas the Jews,' as happened during a protest march in Amsterdam in 2002."[311]

## An abdication of national heritage

The *Washington Post* in September 2015 published a piece entitled "Europe's Fear of Muslim Refugees Echoes Rhetoric of 1930s Antisemitism," likening those concerned about this massive Muslim influx into Europe to Nazis ready to incinerate Jews by the millions.[312] This was a common view, and hand in hand with it went the notion that it was racist, xenophobic, and Islamophobic to oppose what was happening.

On the one hand, there were in Europe migrants who believed, with Dyab Abou Jahjah, that "assimilation was cultural rape." On the other hand, there were native Europeans who thought that Europe didn't have much that was worth assimilating to in the first place. These assumptions led to a scenario that played out in 2018 in Sweden. Some of the people in the latter category appointed Qaisar Mahmood, a Muslim born in Pakistan, to be a member of the Swedish National Heritage Board.

This was an extremely anomalous appointment, since Mahmood readily admitted that he had little knowledge of or interest in Sweden's cultural heritage.[313] But this did not pose a major problem, since despite the "National Heritage Board" name, Mahmood's responsibilities did not actually involve preserving and protecting Sweden's cultural heritage and historical sites at all.

Qaisar Mahmood, who once rode his motorcycle around Sweden in an apparently failed attempt to discover what being Swedish consisted of, used his position on the Swedish National Heritage Board not to highlight and celebrate that heritage, but to downplay Sweden's cultural heritage and history and to create a false narrative that would help compel Swedes to accept mass Muslim migration.[314] He said he didn't want simply to alert people to Viking artifacts and the like, but to use Sweden's history to "create the narrative" that will make Muslim migrants "part of something."[315]

This followed a widely publicized story that gave the impression that Islam had been present in Sweden for over a millennium. In October 2017, a Swedish researcher, Annika Larsson, gained international headlines by claiming that burial costumes from Viking graves dating back to the ninth and tenth centuries had been found to be inscribed with the name "Allah."[316] The intent of this was obvious: to convince Swedes that Islam had always been a part of Sweden, all the way back to the days of the Vikings, and so they should not be concerned about the mass Muslim migration that was now bringing Sweden unprecedented rape and other crime rates.

The Viking burial cloths, however, didn't really feature the name "Allah" at all, as Stephennie Mulder, an associate professor of medieval Islamic art and archaeology at the University of Texas at Austin, proved shortly thereafter, but by then the damage had been done.[317] The idea had entered, however dimly, the popular consciousness: the Vikings were really Muslims. Islam is Swedish. Sweden was Islamic before it was Christian. The Muslim migrants are Swedes.

The "Allah" Viking burial cloth propaganda offensive was one manifestation of what Qaisar Mahmood and others like him were doing. There was no Muslim history in Sweden, but Qaisar Mahmood was working to change the very idea of cultural heritage and fabricate fictions about a historical Muslim presence in Sweden in order to advance his political and sociological agenda.

Mahmood, as a Pakistani, of course had no Swedish heritage of his own. His admitted lack of knowledge of Swedish heritage and history ought to have disqualified him from his position, but this was how Sweden was obliterating itself and committing cultural and national suicide. After all, Swedes appointed Qaisar Mahmood to his job. It was Swedish leaders who wanted to destroy Swedish cultural and national identity.

## Oriana Fallaci, Europe's Cassandra

The celebrated Italian journalist Oriana Fallaci foresaw this wholesale cultural collapse of Europe and tried to stop it—and was put on trial for her trouble.

Fallaci once made presidents and kings and prime ministers shake with fear when they saw her coming to interview them. Ariel Sharon, when she entered his office, quipped, "I see you've come to add another notch to your belt." He had likely heard of Henry Kissinger's comment that his interview with Fallaci was "the most disastrous conversation I ever had with any member of the press."[318]

When she interviewed the Ayatollah Khomeini in 1979, she was forced to wear a chador; during the interview, however, when she complained about the oppression of women in Iran, Khomeini growled, "Our customs are none of your business. If you do not like Islamic dress, you are not obliged to wear it. Because Islamic dress is for good and proper young women."[319] To that, Fallaci replied, "That's very kind of you, Imam. And since you said so, I'm going to take off this stupid, medieval rag right now. There. Done. But tell me something . . ."[320] At that point, Fallaci later recounted, "he got up like a cat, as agile as a cat, an agility I would never expect in a man as old as he was, and he left me. In fact, I had to wait for twenty-four hours (or forty-eight?) to see him again and conclude the interview."[321]

Before she was allowed to continue, Khomeini's son Ahmed told Fallaci that the imam was quite angry over what had happened the previous day, so she had better avoid the subject of chadors. When the interview resumed, Fallaci accordingly asked him immediately about chadors. "First he looked at me in astonishment. Total astonishment. Then his lips moved in a shadow of a smile. Then the shadow of a smile became a real smile. And finally it became a laugh. He laughed, yes. And, when the interview was over, Ahmed whispered to me, 'Believe me, I never saw my father laugh. I think you are the only person in this world who made him laugh.'"[322]

Her reaction to the Islamization of Europe after September 11, 2001, however, did not provoke laughter. In a blaze of righteous anger, she wrote *The Rage and the Pride,* explaining that what hit the U.S. on 9/11 was an age-old enemy who was threatening not just the United States, but also Europe and the entire free world.

*The Rage and the Pride* became a massive bestseller and gained her death threats from Muslims that forced her into hiding. Even then, the Western intelligentsia did not see the writing on the wall but vociferously criticized her book, as well as its follow-up, *The Force of Reason*, in which she wrote, "This time I do not appeal to rage, to pride. I do not even appeal to passion. I appeal to Reason."[323] (There were some notable exceptions: the Center for the Study of Popular Culture, later to be known as the David Horowitz Freedom Center, awarded her its Annie Taylor Award for courage under fire on November 28, 2005.) Nor did they limit themselves just to criticism. Oriana Fallaci was one of the most fearless and courageous defenders Western civilization had in these latter days, and the West rewarded her by hounding, persecuting, and vilifying her.

When Fallaci was 75 years old and dying of cancer, Italian authorities attempted to put her on trial for "defaming Islam." The complaint came from an Italian convert to Islam with the unlikely name of Adel Smith. Smith, president of the Muslim Union of Italy, who was never charged with defaming Christianity after he referred to a crucifix as a "miniature cadaver" during his efforts to have depictions of Christ on the Cross removed from Italian schools.[324]

Smith amassed a reputation as something of a crank after demanding that Christians deny aspects of their faith that offended his Islamic sensibilities: he called for the destruction of Giovanni da Modena's fresco *The Last Judgment* in the 14th-century cathedral of San Petronio in Bologna, Italy, because that priceless expression of Medieval Christianity depicts the Muslim Prophet Muhammad in hell.[325] And in the mother of all frivolous lawsuits, Smith in February 2004 brought suit against Pope John Paul II and Joseph Cardinal Ratzinger, who later became Pope Benedict XVI, for offending Islam by expressing in various writings their opinion, utterly unremarkable from two Christian leaders, that Christianity is unique and preferable to other religions, including Islam.[326]

Smith's suit against Fallaci was hardly less frivolous, but he was able to find a judge willing to play along. Judge Armando Grasso of Bergamo, Italy, ruled that *The Force of Reason* contained 18 statements "unequivocally offensive to Islam and Muslims," and that therefore she had to be tried.[327] Smith exulted at Grasso's decision: "It is the first time a judge has ordered a trial for defamation of the Islamic faith. But this isn't just about defamation. We would also like (the court) to recognize that this is an incitement to religious hatred."[328]

Fallaci remarked of the indictment: "When I was given the news, I laughed. Bitterly, of course, but I laughed. No amusement, no surprise, because the trial is nothing else but a demonstration that everything I've written is true."[329] The trial was set for June 2006, but Fallaci, by then living in New York City, made no plans to attend, saying in June 2005, "I don't even know if I will be around next year. My cancers are so bad that I think I've arrived at the end of the road. What a pity. I would like to live not only because I love life so much, but because I'd like to see the result of the trial. I do think I will be found guilty."[330] At a preliminary hearing in June 2006, a judge ruled that Fallaci should indeed stand trial, and set that trial for December 18 of that year.[331] Fallaci died on September 15, 2006, in Florence.

*The Guardian,* in its obituary, termed her "notorious for her Islamophobia."[332] The British sociologist Chris Allen, in his 2013 book *Islamophobia,* criticized her for "inferring that Islam should not be in 'our' lands what with it being indeterminably Other."[333] Another book published that same year blamed her for helping create and reinforce "an anti-Islamic Zeitgeist that has developed and reinvented the assortment of stereotypes about the 'migration question' and generated a specific xenophobia against Muslims."[334] In 2014, an attempt to name a street in Rome after Fallaci ran afoul of two Italian leftist political parties, the Democratic Party (PD) and the Left Ecology Freedom (Sel), which complained that her writings contained "religious hatred."[335]

This leftist line on Oriana Fallaci and her work hasn't changed, for the Muslim migrant crisis in Europe made it abundantly clear, as if there had been any real doubt before then, that Fallaci had been right all along. If her words had been heeded 10 years ago, the severe crisis that Europe now faces might have been averted. Instead, she stands as a new Cassandra, unheeded but vindicated.

Even Christopher Hitchens, who himself faced accusations of "Islamophobia" for writing honestly about the jihad threat, criticized *The Rage and the Pride* as "a sort of primer in how not to write about Islam," skewering its "obsessive interest in excrement, disease, sexual mania, and insectlike reproduction, insofar as these apply to Muslims in general and to Muslim immigrants in Europe in particular."[336]

Lurid indeed. And in *The Force of Reason,* Fallaci wrote about "the so-called Policy-of-the-Womb, I mean the strategy of exporting human beings and having them breed in abundance," which she dubbed "the simplest way to take possession of a territory. To dominate a country, to replace a population or to subjugate it. And, from the Eighth Century onwards, Islamic expansionism has often unfolded in the shadow of that strategy. Often, through rape and concubinage."[337]

Fallaci would accordingly not have been surprised the huge number of sex assaults and gang rapes that were committed by Muslim migrants all over Europe, or at the official coverups of what was happening. In *The Force of Reason,* Fallaci likened herself to Maestro Cecco, who was burned at the stake for running afoul of the Inquisition. She pointed out that European authorities had not changed, and in modern times, a new Inquisition was intent on defending not Catholicism, but Islam, at all costs, and persecuting those who dared raise their voices against the conquest and Islamization of the continent. She would with mordant wit excoriate European officials' reaction to the sex assaults—after all, she saw it coming.

Fallaci would not have been surprised, either, to see that the first response of European authorities to the mass sex assaults was to try to cover them up. Speaking on a related issue, the high Muslim birthrate as compared to that of native Europeans, she wrote, "Ah! Touching this subject means risking more than pillory and harassment. It means asking for a life sentence. In our subjugated Europe the Islamic fertility is such a taboo that nobody ever dares to speak about it. If you try, you go straight to court for racism and xenophobia and blasphemy."[338]

This was the new Europe that Fallaci foresaw and tried to stave off. "Europe is no longer Europe," she wrote: "it is Eurabia, a colony of Islam, where the Islamic invasion does not proceed only in a physical sense, but also in a mental and cultural sense."[339]

Islamic jihadis had made their intention to exploit the migrant crisis abundantly clear. In February 2015, the Islamic State boasted it would soon flood Europe with as many as 500,000 refugees.[340] The intention was not just to overwhelm Europe's humanitarian apparatus, although that played a role; the main goal was to send jihadis into Europe among peaceful migrants and refugees.

That September, when the migrant influx into Europe had begun, Lebanese Education Minister Elias Bou Saab said that there were 20,000 jihadis among the refugees in camps in his country.[341] Meanwhile, 80% of migrants who have recently come to Europe claiming to be fleeing the war in Syria aren't really from Syria at all, strongly suggesting that the purpose of this migration is not, contrary to universal assumption, to flee a war zone.[342]

## *The supremacy of Islamic law in Europe*

Late in September 2019, French politician Marion Maréchal described France's "first major challenge, the most vital," as "the Great Replacement, this demographic countdown, which already makes us realise the possibility of becoming a minority on the land of our ancestors." A multicultural society in France, she said, would be "fractured and violent," and she noted that France in many ways had already changed beyond recognition: "After 40 years of mass migration, Islamic lobbies and political correctness, France is in the process of passing from the eldest daughter of the Catholic Church, to becoming the little niece of Islam. Terrorism is only the tip of the iceberg—this is not the France that our grandparents fought for."[343]

Maréchal had a point. Special accommodation of Muslim sensibilities has become the cultural norm in Europe. Often, Muslims don't even need to complain: the solicitude for their feelings has been so thoroughly inculcated in the European populace that it regularly trumps free speech. In November 2015 in Italy, a school headmaster, Marco Parma of the Garofani school in Rozano, seeing offense to Muslims in a hallowed Christian practice, canceled the school's annual Christmas carol concert. Explained Parma, "I believe that respecting the sensitivities of people of different religions or cultures is a step forward towards integration," he said. "This is a multiethnic school."[344]

What about the sensitivities of Italians who wanted to sing Christmas carols? Parma didn't address them, but in the storm of indignation that followed, Parma was forced to resign. By the next summer, however, as Muslim migrants flooded into Italy, attitudes had changed—at least among some Italians. In the summer of 2016, even Christian prayer in a Christian church was deemed offensive to Muslims. Members of the Catholic charity Caritas told parishioners at St. Anthony church in Ventimiglia not to recite the rosary aloud, but to pray in silence so as not to offend the Muslim migrants who were being housed at the church.[345]

The result of this relativism was an increasing acceptance of Sharia provisions that contradicted European laws and traditions. Polygamy remains illegal in Spain as of this writing, but in January 2020, the Spanish supreme court awarded the two widows of a Moroccan Muslim migrant who died in Spain in 2012 the right to collect widows' pensions. The court explained that polygamy's illegal status did not preclude the right to receive a pension, as both women were legally married to the man, and that was all that was needed for them to collect the pension money. This opened the door to the legalization of polygamy and legal recognition of other aspects of Sharia as well.

The Spanish supreme court's ruling in this case set an important precedent. Its ruling overruled that of the Superior Court of Justice of Madrid, which had declared that one of the widows was ineligible. The supreme court's ruling reinforced its ruling in a 2018 case involving another Moroccan Muslim migrant who died leaving behind two widows, in which it ruled the same way.

Demonstrating yet again the correctness of Bat Ye'or's observation that the seeds of the present crisis in Europe were planted decades ago, the supreme court in its decision made reference to Article 23 of the Social Security Agreement that Spain and Morocco entered into in November 1979. That Agreement stipulated that "the widowhood pension caused by a Moroccan worker will be distributed, where appropriate, equally and definitely among those who turn out to be, according to Moroccan legislation, beneficiaries of said benefit."[346]

## The death of free speech in Europe

In majority-Muslim countries, restrictions on certain types of speech and expression are routine. In January 2007 in Qatar, a man went to the Saudi-owned Jarir Bookstore and bought a Winnie the Pooh book for his daughter, only to find that someone had carefully gone through every page and blacked out Pooh's friend Piglet—lest any young Muslims developing Islamic sensibilities be offended by the sight of a cartoon of an animal deemed unclean by Islamic law.[347]

This kind of thing happens even in Muslim countries that are widely reputed to be moderate. In Malaysia in 2014, KHL Printing Company, the local printer of the *International New York Times*, blackened out images of the faces of pigs in two photos. A KHL employee explained, "This is a Muslim country so we covered the pigs' eyes. We usually do that for the *International New York Times*—also for pictures of cigarettes, weapons, guns and nude pictures."[348]

Such censorship has long been taken for granted in Muslim countries. But now it has arrived in Europe.

"When this great writer resorts to outrageous stigmatization of Islam, the limits of what is tolerable are breached": in June 2002, the Islamic Center of Geneva called for *The Rage and the Pride* to be banned. Swiss Muslim leader Hani Ramadan, grandson of Muslim Brotherhood founder Hassan al-Banna, claimed that Fallaci was "insulting the Muslim community as a whole with her shameful words."[349]

Compliant Swiss authorities tried to have Fallaci extradited to Switzerland to face trial, but failed.[350] The Movement against Racism and for Friendship between Peoples (MRAP) in France declared, "Freedom of expression is and will remain a fundamental right . . . but when this great writer [Fallaci] resorts to outrageous stigmatization of Islam, the limits of what is tolerable are breached."[351]

Clearly the real religious hatred in Europe was coming from other quarters. But no matter how much hostility European Muslims expressed towards non-Muslim culture in general and Christianity in particular, they appeared to be immune from charges that they were engaging in "hate speech."

Pope Francis certainly seemed to have assumed so. Fallaci wrote in *The Force of Reason* about "the Catholic Church without which the Islamization of Europe, and the degeneration of Europe into Eurabia, could never have developed."[352] She wrote passionately against "this Catholic Church that remains silent even when the crucifix gets insulted, derided, expelled from hospitals. This Catholic Church that never roars against their polygamy and wife-repudiation and slavery. Because in Islam slavery is not a foul stain of the past, my dear priests and bishops and cardinals who preach to love the enemy."[353]

Fallaci would have been appalled by Pope Francis, who so indefatigably preached "to love the enemy" that he appears to have equated that love with cultural and civilizational surrender. Pope Francis has called strongly and repeatedly for Europe to open its doors to massive and unrestricted Muslim migration, despite the demonstrable jihad terror threat that the migrants pose, as well as the difficulty European nations will inevitably have in integrating massive new populations that believe that Islamic society and law are superior and preferable to European models. His mindset was epitomized by an April 2016 incident, when a Christian brother and sister who had come to Europe from Syria as refugees were included, or so they were promised, in a group that the Pope planned to bring to Rome. Francis then reneged, however, and took only Muslims with him back to Rome.[354]

## "Allah weet het beter"

In May 2002, a Dutchman named Volkert van der Graaf shot dead the Dutch politician Pim Fortuyn. Although the mainstream media described van der Graaf as an "animal rights activist," the killer himself explained that he "did it for Dutch Muslims," in view of Fortuyn's outspoken criticism of Islam and opposition to mass Muslim immigration into the Netherlands.[355]

Fortuyn's friend Theo van Gogh, a prominent Dutch intellectual and great-grand-nephew of the famous painter, did not share van der Graaf's solicitude for Muslims in the Netherlands. After Fortuyn's death, he became a prominent critic of Islam, penning a book, *Allah weet het beter (Allah Knows*

*Better*), in 2003, and a film, *Submission*, in 2004, which graphically illustrated the plight of women under Islamic law by showing near-naked women with Qur'an verses (in the original Arabic) written on their bodies.

In post-Rushdie Europe, it was perhaps inevitable that van Gogh would receive death threats over *Submission*, but he waved them away, saying that the film itself was "the best protection I could have. It's not something I worry about."[356]

And so it happened on a street in Amsterdam on November 2, 2004. A devout Muslim named Mohammed Bouyeri spotted van Gogh riding on his bicycle, took out a gun, and opened fire. When van Gogh fell to the ground, Bouyeri came running up and began to behead him. In his death throes, van Gogh spoke his last words—words that, if the West surrenders entirely to the global jihad and adopts Islamic blasphemy laws, will serve as the epitaph to free societies: "Can't we talk about this?"[357]

The answer was no, but Bouyeri said nothing. His only reply was to stab van Gogh with his bloody knife, having attached a note to the blade. The note contained quotations from the Qur'an and threats to others in the Netherlands whom Bouyeri deemed to have offended Islam. Van Gogh's collaborator on *Submission*, the Somali ex-Muslim Ayaan Hirsi Ali, later recounted, "The letter was addressed to me," telling her that van Gogh had been "executed" for his blasphemous film, and that she would soon be "executed" as well, for her apostasy.[358]

Studiously ignoring the facts of Theo van Gogh's murder, engaging in self-censorship, and foreshadowing what was to become the default response of officials to every jihad attack in the West, Dutch Prime Minister Jan Peter Balkenende announced that "nothing is known about the motive" of the murderer.[359]

At his trial, Bouyeri flaunted his certainty of his own righteousness. Clutching a copy of the Qur'an, he declared,

> I did what I did purely out my beliefs. I want you to know that I acted out of conviction and not that I took his life because he was Dutch or because I was Moroccan and felt insulted. . . . If I ever get free, I would do it again. . . . What moved me to do what I did was purely my faith. I was motivated by the law that commands me to cut off the head of anyone who insults Allah and his prophet.[360]

He even told van Gogh's grieving mother, "I don't feel your pain. I don't have any sympathy for you. I can't feel for you because I think you're a non-believer."[361]

Testifying in 2007 at the trial of seven accused jihad terrorists, Bouyeri was asked how a Muslim should respond to someone who insults Islam. He replied, "Off with his head. Slaughter him."[362]

## "Freedom of speech is a cornerstone of the EU's order"

In the face of this horrific attack on the freedom of speech, some Western officials came to the defense of this core principle of any free society. Amsterdam mayor Job Cohen declared, "We will show loud and clear that freedom of speech is important to us."[363]

Two years later, European Commission spokesman Johannes Laitenberger would say, "[F]reedom of speech is a cornerstone of the EU's order as is the freedom and respect of all religions and beliefs, be it Christianity, Islam, Judaism, Buddhism or laicism."[364]

The battle was on: it was free expression versus *Allah weet het beter*. But the "Allah knows better" faction was making steady advances all over Europe.

If the freedom of speech was really a cornerstone of the EU's order, it had a funny way of showing it. In January 2009, Austrian politician Susanne Winter was fined €24,000 ($31,000) for opining that "in today's system," Muhammad would be classified as a "child molester" for marrying a six-year-old girl and consummating the marriage when she was nine, and for criticizing what she called an "Islamic immigration tsunami."[365]

The truth was no defense. It didn't matter in the least that Islamic tradition itself says Muhammad "married Aisha when she was a girl of six years of age, and he consummated that marriage when she was nine years old."[366] He was at this time 54 years old. Islamic tradition also depicts Aisha herself recounting that she was six when Muhammad married her and nine when he took her into his household:

> My mother, Umm Ruman, came to me while I was playing in a swing with some of my girl friends. She called me, and I went to her, not knowing what she wanted to do to me. She caught me by the hand and made me stand at the door of the house. I was breathless then, and when my breathing became normal, she took some water and rubbed my face and head with it. Then she took me into the house.

There in the house I saw some Ansari [recent Muslim converts] women who said, "Best wishes and Allah's Blessing and a good luck." Then she entrusted me to them and they prepared me (for the marriage). Unexpectedly Allah's Messenger came to me in the forenoon and my mother handed me over to him, and at that time I was a girl of nine years of age.[367]

But none of that mattered at the trials of Winter and another Austrian, human rights activist Elisabeth Sabaditsch-Wolff. In November 2009, Sabaditsch-Wolff gave a seminar about Islam at a political academy known as the Freedom Education Institute. A socialist magazine in Austria called *NEWS* secretly recorded two of her lectures and then had her charged with hate speech.[368]

There was just one problem: Sabaditsch-Wolff hadn't actually engaged in any "hate speech"; her lectures were largely made up of quotations from the Qur'an and other Islamic sources. But even when it became clear that the charge was baseless, Judge Bettina Neubauer didn't dismiss the case, instead she simply suspended the hearings until January 18, 2011—at which point Neubauer told Sabaditsch-Wolff that she was now being charged not only with hate speech, but with "denigration of religious beliefs of a legally recognized religion."[369] Sabaditsch-Wolff was duly found guilty of the latter charge.[370]

Sabaditsch-Wolff was guilty, Neubauer explained, because she had said that Muhammad, the prophet of Islam, "had a thing for little girls."[371] This constituted denigration because while Muhammad consummated his marriage with a nine-year-old girl when he was 54, Islamic sources did not record that he ever showed any interest in other prepubescent girls, and also had adult wives at the same time, so it was false and defamatory to say that he was a pedophile.

Sabaditsch-Wolff was fined €480 ($625) plus the costs of the trial.[372] Her conviction, she said, was "a black day for Austria." The Vienna Federation of Academics called Neubauer's decision 'politically and sentimentally motivated justice" that meant "the end of freedom of expression in Austria."[373]

## "The price that we all have to pay for this freedom is that others have a right to criticize our politics, our religion and our culture"

Lars Hedegaard, writer, free speech activist, and president of the Danish Free Press Society, was also put on trial for "hate speech" for noting in a

December 2009 interview that there were high rates of child rape and wife-beating among Muslims. Although this was true, Hedegaard was charged under Article 266b of the Danish penal code, which mandates a fine or imprisonment for up to two years for anyone who "publicly or with the intent of public dissemination issues a pronouncement or other communication by which a group of persons are threatened, insulted or denigrated due to their race, skin color, national or ethnic origin, religion or sexual orientation."[374]

Hedegaard's legal ordeal went on for several years, with his persecutors claiming that his remarks suggested that all Muslims were child molesters and wife beaters. He was acquitted in January 2011, but prosecutors appealed, and a superior court found him guilty in May 2011. His case made it all the way to the Danish Supreme Court, where Hedegaard delivered an eloquent defense of the freedom of speech in connection with Islam.

In April 2012, the Danish Supreme Court acquitted Hedegaard on a technicality. While declaring that his statements did indeed violate Danish law, the court ruled that Hedegaard had not been proven to have made them "publicly," as he wasn't aware that his remarks would be published. Hedegaard was "pleased that the Supreme Court has handed down a judgment in accordance with the evidence that was presented in the District Court and High Court," but he noted the ominous implications: "This judgment cannot be interpreted as a victory for freedom of speech. Article 266b, under which I was charged, remains unchanged. It remains a disgrace to any civilized society and is an open invitation to frivolous trials. Thus, we still have no right to refer to truth if we are indicted under this article."[375]

## "Destroying our country"

The persecutions of Fallaci, Wilders, Winter, Sabaditsch-Wolff, and Hedegaard were the highest-profile free speech cases in Europe, but there were others:

*France*: Michel Houellebecq, a novelist, was prosecuted but ultimately acquitted in 2002 for saying that Islam was "the stupidest religion" and that the Qur'an was "badly written."[376] Even literary criticism was apparently now "hate speech."

*France*: Brigitte Bardot, the film legend, was charged with "inciting racial hatred" for making statements critical of Muslims and Islam and was found guilty no fewer than five times. In June 2008, she was given a fine of €15,000 (around $23,000) for observing that Muslims in France were "destroying our country."[377] No one seems to have dared to point out that what was really destroying the country were fines of that size for speech that was considered beyond the bounds of acceptable discourse.

*France*: In 2010, writer Renaud Camus gave a speech about how multiculturalism was a Trojan Horse for the French people. He was convicted of "Islamophobia" and fined €4,000.[378]

*France*: Marie Laforêt, a singer and actress, was prosecuted in 2011 over a job advertisement she placed on an Internet website. The ad said that "people with allergies or orthodox Muslims" need not apply—because she owned a dog. Dogs are considered unclean under Islamic law.[379]

*The Netherlands*: Gregorius Nekschot, a satirical cartoonist, was arrested in 2008 for cartoons that Dutch authorities thought were offensive to Muslims. The charges were thrown out in 2010, but Nekschot, weary of the ordeal, stopped drawing cartoons.[380]

*Denmark*: Jesper Langballe, a Member of Parliament, was convicted of hate speech in 2010 for noting (correctly) that among Muslim families, honor killings and sex abuse are disturbingly common. Truth is no defense in Denmark.[381]

*Finland*: Jussi Kristian Halla-aho, a politician, was charged in 2009 with "incitement against an ethnic group" and "breach of the sanctity of religion" for saying that Islam was a religion of pedophilia—a reasonable assertion in light of the facts that Muhammad did consummate his marriage with a nine-year-old when he was 54 and that his example is the model for normative Muslim behavior.[382]

Those who dared to speak out against jihad terror and Islamic supremacism in Europe didn't face challenges only from legal authorities and Islamic jihadists. There was also self-censorship on the part of publishers. The French translation of ex-Muslim Hamed Abdel-Samad's book *Der islamische Faschismus: Eine Analyse* (*Islamic Fascism: An Analysis*) was dropped at the last minute by its publisher, Piranha, not just because of threats, but because the book would aid the "extreme right."[383] And in Germany, novelist Gabriele Brinkmann lost the publisher of her novel *Wem Ehre geburt* (*To Whom Honor Gives Birth*) because the book could be seen as "insulting to Muslims."[384]

# CHAPTER 6

## ERDOGAN AND MIGRATION AS A WEAPON

### *Visa-free travel, or else*

The migrant influx and the cultural aggression of many migrants was certainly aided and abetted by Europe's cultural collapse and self-hatred, but it was also bolstered by pressures from outside the continent. Most notably, Turkish President Recep Tayyip Erdogan used the migrant crisis as a weapon to force Europe to do his bidding.

After a failed coup against Erdogan, European Union officials in May 2016 expressed concerns that Turkey's anti-terrorism laws were so broad that they could be used to crush dissent against the Erdogan regime and asked the Turkish government to change these laws as part of an agreement to reduce the migrant flow into Europe. Turkey's minister for EU affairs, Volkan Bozkir, rejected these requests, saying flatly, "It is not possible for us to accept any changes to the counter-terrorism law."[385] Erdogan bluntly told the European Union, "We're going our way, you go yours."[386]

Meanwhile, a close adviser to Erdogan, Burhan Kuzu, issued a threat, tying the migrant influx to Turkish citizens being granted visa-free travel throughout the European Union: "The European Parliament will discuss the report that will open Europe visa-free for Turkish citizens. If the wrong decision is taken, we will send the refugees."[387]

In April 2017, a Turkish referendum granted Erdogan sweeping new powers. A week before the vote, Erdogan played the victim card, claiming that Turkish migrants in Europe were "oppressed" and "humiliated."[388] He warned, "Europe will pay for what they have done. ... They said a century ago that we were the 'sick man.' Now they are the 'sick man.' Europe is collapsing."[389]

European officials feared that an emboldened Erdogan would renew the threat that he would flood Europe with Muslim migrants unless the EU granted Turks visa-free travel. A senior Greek official expressed these fears: "There was a lot of steamy, bellicose rhetoric made by Erdogan ahead of the referendum. If he continues with belligerent policies then Greece will be the first to face the fallout. The fear is real but the question is whether Erdogan will risk turning into a regional pariah."[390]

The fears were not unfounded. Turkey's Foreign Minister Mevlut Cavusoglu warned that the country would consider its agreement with the European Union regarding the migrants, which kept most of them out of Europe, to be no longer in effect unless Turks were granted this free movement. Italian MEP Gianni Pittella noted, "We've always been very reluctant to ensure a visa-free regime to Turkey as, in our opinion, Ankara does not match the democratic criteria. Now after the referendum our concerns are even bigger."[391]

Turkey's minister for EU affairs, Omer Celik, again rejected EU requests that Turkey alter its anti-terror legislation in order to make anti-terror laws more difficult to use against opponents of the regime, using European anti-terror laws as a pretext: "While legislation is being aggravated and strengthened in the face of terrorist threats across Europe, it is unrealistic to expect that Turkey should weaken its legislation."[392]

A month before this, Erdogan framed his conflict with Europe as a revival of the wars between the warriors of Christianity and Islam that had preoccupied the continent for a millennium. After the European Court of Justice upheld the dismissal of the case of two Muslim women who defied anti-hijab laws, Erdogan fumed: "Shame on the EU. Down with your European principles, values and justice. They started a clash between the cross and the crescent, there is no other explanation."[393]

Erdogan returned to this theme in June 2018, when the government of Austria moved to expel imams who preached or abetted jihad terror and close their mosques. Erdogan said, "These measures taken by the Austrian prime minister are, I fear, leading the world toward a war between the cross and the crescent."[394]

Then, in October 2019, after Turkish armies moved into Syria to fight Kurdish forces that Turkey had long labeled terrorist groups, Erdogan harangued, "Hey European Union. Pull yourself together," adding, "I say it again. If you try to label this operation as an invasion, it's very simple: we will open the gates and send 3.6 million refugees your way."[395]

Meeting in November 2019 with Hungarian Prime Minister Viktor Orban, who has opposed the mass migrant influx, Erdogan renewed his threats, once again in the context of demanding additional aid from the European Union. "Whether or not support comes," Erdogan declared, "we will continue to host our guests, but only up to a point." The "guests" to which he was referring were Muslim migrants from all over the Islamic world. "If we see that this does not work," he continued, "just like I said before, we will have no option left but to open the gates. If we open the gates, it is obvious where they will go."[396]

## Making good on the threats

On February 27, 2020, Erdogan made good on these threats, announcing that he would for the next 72 hours allow any and all migrants in Syria to pass through Turkey into Europe. Turkish journalist Ragip Soylu stated, "Land and sea crossings to Europe would be free to pass for the NEXT 72 HOURS and Turkey will open the borders immediately."[397] This followed Erdogan's demand for aid from Europe to build a "security zone" for migrants along Turkey's border with Syria: "Give us logistical support, and we can build houses up to 30 kilometres into the north of Syria. Either that happens, or we open the gates."[398] EU spokeswoman Natasha Bertaud said that by September 2019, the EU had already given Turkey €5.6 billion ($6 billion) under the terms of their migrant pact.[399]

On March 2, 2020, Erdogan boasted, "After we opened the doors, there were multiple calls saying 'close the doors.' I told them 'it's done. It's finished. The doors are now open. Now, you will have to take your share of the burden.' Since we have opened the borders, the number of refugees heading toward Europe has reached hundreds of thousands. This number will soon be in the millions."[400]

In early March 2020, the Greek government released a video showing that the Erdogan government had entirely engineered the migrant crisis at the border. According to the video, the Turkish government on February 28 opened the border and "systematically encourage[d] and assist[ed] migrants to reach the Greek border."[401] One migrant exclaimed, "President Erdogan has arranged for free rides [to the border], Allah bless his soul," and "The [Turkish] authorities drove us to the border and told us to cross."[402] One of the migrants had been a prisoner, and recounted: "Police let us out . . . [and] brought us here and told us that the gates are opened."[403]

Migrants used tear gas supplied by the Turkish government to try to break through the border, throwing rocks and using trees as battering rams, while screaming "Allahu Akbar!"[404]

While all this was going on, Erdogan also held out the possibility of a normalization of relations, but only on his terms, saying on March 12,

"Implementing the truce in Idlib and finding a permanent solution to the refugee problem is for everyone's benefit. We can start a new era with the EU. If the EU shows this determination and political vision, it is possible to go the distance."[405] By "determination and political vision," Erdogan clearly meant acceptance of his entire agenda, as in the same speech he castigated Greek Prime Minister Kyriakos Mitsotakis for not allowing the migrants free entry: "Greece," Erdogan claimed, "is not aware of International Law. Mitsotakis must first learn International Law. He should read the Universal Declaration of Human Rights."[406] And he called upon Greeks to bend to his demands: "Hey Greece! I appeal to you . . . open the gates as well and be free of this burden. . . . Let them go to other European countries."[407]

Erdogan wasn't alone in seeing the migrant influx into European as a weapon to force the European Union to do his bidding. Echoing the bellicose Turkish President, a lawmaker in Lebanon named Mohammad Raed boasted, "All we have to do is wave the card of Syrian refugees and all the European countries will kneel before us."[408]

This longstanding campaign of intimidation worked. The European Commission in March 2020 agreed to give Turkey €500 million ($539,400,000) above and beyond the financial aid it had already committed to the Turkish regime in order to aid "Syrian refugees."[409] Turkey was to receive this windfall regardless of the fact that most of the migrants who had been trying to break through Greek border defenses and make their way to Western Europe were neither Syrians or refugees. Voice of Europe reported that of 252 people who were arrested while trying to enter Greece illegally from Turkey, only a tiny minority were actually Syrian: "64 percent were Afghani, 19 percent were Pakistani, 5 percent were Turkish, 4 percent were Syrian, 2.6 percent were Somalian, and those from Iraq, Iran, Morocco, Ethiopia, Bangladesh, and Egypt comprised 5.4 percent of the arrestees."[410]

Many of these migrants had been lured to Europe by false promises, promises that had not come from European authorities. One Moroccan migrant recounted: "We saw on WhatsApp and Facebook messages that say the doors are open between Turkey and Greece. So we came to try to go to France, or to Germany. We have nothing in Morocco, no work, no money, I don't want to stay at home doing nothing."[411]

The Turkish government may have been the source of this misinformation, as Turkish officials were actively aiding the migrants to get to the Greek border, and even giving them tear gas to fight back against Greek forces that barred their entry. Greek government spokesman Stelios Petsas charged the Turkish government with orchestrating the entire migrant crisis.

As the coronavirus pandemic engulfed the world later in March 2020, Erdogan withdrew his migrants from the Greek border. Turkish Interior Minister Suleyman Soylu announced that Turkish authorities had moved 5,800 migrants away from the border. "It was a precautionary move," he explained.[412] "We had to do it. But no one has yet to feel comfortable with it."[413] He emphasized that his government's policies had not changed, and that they could return: "When this epidemic is over we would not prevent whoever wants to leave."[414] Where they would go was not in doubt: "When the coronavirus pandemic is over, we are not going to deter any immigrants who want to return to the Greek–Turkish border in Pazar."[415]

Nonetheless, the Greek government termed the withdrawal an "important thing for our country and for Europe."[416] Greek Prime Minister Kyriakos Mitsotakis said, "A chapter might potentially be closing, but this battle, have no doubt, continues."[417] He added, "We managed to secure a very important thing for our country and for Europe. The ability and efficiency of guarding our land and sea borders."[418]

There was little doubt, however, that those borders would be tested again. George Koumoutsakos, Greece's Deputy Foreign Minister, declared that the "statements by Soyilu respond to those who still had the slightest doubt that the events in Evros were an aggressive plan to brutally blackmail Greece and Europe with a 'weapon' of migrant exploitation."[419]

## No assimilation

Meanwhile, Erdogan told Muslim migrants who were already in Europe not to assimilate into European society. As far back as 2008, while serving as Prime Minister of Turkey, Erdogan told migrants, "Nobody can expect you to submit to assimilation. Assimilation is a crime against humanity!"[420] In February 2011, he said the same thing to an adoring crowd of thousands of Turkish immigrants in Germany. As they waited for Erdogan, a song played with the lyric, "The land belongs to us all."[421] The migrants made clear that they meant their old land, the values and mores of which they were bringing to their new home, as they chanted, "Turkey is great!"[422] One migrant in the crowd exulted, "The Germans will never accept us, but we have Erdogan." Another stated, "At last someone feels responsible for us, for the first time a Turkish prime minister isn't forgetting his compatriots abroad."[423]

In his address, Erdogan made it clear to the crowd that they were still part of Turkey: "They call you guest workers, foreigners, or German Turks. It doesn't matter what they all call you: You are my fellow citizens, you are my people, you are my friends, you are my brothers and sisters! You are part of Germany, but you are also part our great Turkey."[424] He made it clear which of these allegiances should be paramount when he told them, "Yes, integrate yourselves into German society but don't assimilate yourselves. No one has the right to deprive us of our culture and our identity."[425]

And speaking in December 2019 to Turkish migrants in Switzerland, the Turkish President emphasized their identity as Turks, exclaiming, "One nation, one flag, one home, one state. So we continue!"[426] At the same time, he told them to get involved in Swiss society: "Get active, in politics, science, the economy!"[427]

# CHAPTER 7

## THE RISE OF POPULISM IN WESTERN EUROPE—AND THE REACTION TO IT

### *The rise of European populism*

S
ome people in Europe were not willing to go quietly into the night of jihad violence, civil strife, Sharia, and Islamization. The political elites, anxious to preserve their places of privilege and power, immediately turned on these defenders of the continent, identifying them as the real threat to the stability and prosperity of the European Union countries. The American pundit David Frum summed up the views of many among the old guard in Europe and North America when he wrote in November 2018, "When I was young, the most important challenges to those free societies seemed to come from Communists and Marxists. When I was not so young, the most important of those challenges seemed to come from Islamists. Today, they seem to come from—again, speaking politely—populists."[428]

In Germany, the North Rhine-Westphalia state government spent $557,000 of taxpayer funds on a series of videos that began running on a YouTube channel in August 2019. The channel, the state's Interior Ministry explained, "satirically addresses the absurdity of radicalization, terrorism and Islamism."[429] According to Deutsche Welle, "one satire shows a right-wing populist and an Islamic extremist bonding over sexism and homophobia while trying to convert passersby."[430] The videos were directed toward young Muslims, trying to dissuade them from turning to jihad. That fact made it clear that this video meant to shame viewers into refraining from joining a jihad group out of a fear of becoming like "right-wing populists." The North Rhine-Westphalia government was making the error of assuming that the jihadis shared their worldview and basic assumptions. They didn't. But the project demonstrated, if nothing else, how negatively some German authorities viewed the populists.

The reason for this negative view was clear: the populists challenged everything upon which the elites had staked the future of Europe. In April 2019, some of Europe's leading populists addressed a rally in Prague, several weeks before elections for the European Parliament. France's Marine Le Pen declared, "The battle of Europe has begun."[431] Blaming the EU for the mass migration into the continent, she cried out, "Long live a Europe of sovereign nations."[432] The Netherlands' Geert Wilders stated that the EU was trying to "erase our nation states," and added, "Today, we're fighting for our existence."[433] He maintained that there was an unavoidable conflict between Islamic values and those of Europe: "Islam is a medieval cult that denies freedom to others. Islam and freedom are not compatible."[434]

The populist movement in Europe developed over the first two decades of the 21st century. In the early 2000s, the Dutch politician Pim Fortuyn, who was openly gay and whose kitchen featured portraits of Marx and Lenin, earned one of the establishment media's favorite terms of opprobrium: "far right." Fortuyn held only one position that earned him that label: he maintained the incompatibility of traditional Islamic values with the liberal, secular societies of the West.

Fortuyn's homosexuality led him to this. "I have gay friends," he explained, "who have been beaten up by young Moroccans in Rotterdam."[435] He noted that Muslims had belittled and insulted him, saying that, as a gay man, he was "lower than a pig."[436] He called Islam "backward" and asserted that "Christianity and Judaism have gone through the laundromat of humanism and enlightenment, but that isn't the case with Islam."[437] He pointed out that "in Holland homosexuality is treated the same way as heterosexuality. In what Islamic country does that happen?"[438]

Fortuyn proposed curbs on Muslim immigration to Holland and called for the assimilation of the Muslims already in the Netherlands into the secular, multiethnic, multicultural, tolerant framework of modern Dutch society. "We need to integrate these people; they need to accept that, in Holland, gender equality and tolerance of different lifestyle is very, very important to us."[439]

In May 2002, Fortuyn was murdered by a non-Muslim Dutchman named Volkert van der Graaf, who explained, "I shot Fortuyn for Dutch Muslims."[440] Van der Graaf charged that Fortuyn was making Dutch Muslims into "scapegoats," and that he was exploiting "the weak parts of society to score points."[441] Van der Graaf compared Fortuyn's rise to that of Adolf Hitler, and portrayed the shooting as a noble attempt to save the Netherlands from the far right.[442] He planned his crime carefully and shot Fortuyn six times, for which he received the astonishingly lenient sentence of 18 years in prison.[443] Perhaps the prevailing sentiment in Europe that Muslims there were an oppressed minority contributed to van der Graaf's light sentencing.

Yet Fortuyn's points were proven true again and again. Several months after he was murdered, another gay politician, Paris Mayor Bertrand Delanoe, was stabbed by a "devout Muslim" who "acted out of opposition to politicians and gays."[444] While Fortuyn still lived, Khalil el-Moumni, a prominent imam in Rotterdam, sparked a national controversy in Holland by calling homosexuality a "sickness" and saying, "Homosexuality does not remain restricted to the people who have this disease. If this disease spreads, everyone could become infected."[445]

## *"In a democratic system, hate speech is considered so serious that it is in the general interest to . . . draw a clear line"*

Another Dutch politician, Geert Wilders, was the leader of the Party for Freedom, the first longstanding and successful populist movement in Europe. Wilders became nationally and internationally prominent after Fortuyn's death. He became a member of the Dutch Parliament while maintaining the incompatibility of Sharia with Western laws, values, and mores. That position, as well as his short film *Fitna* that so aroused the ire of the OIC, earned him so many death threats from Muslims that he was placed under 24-hour guard, began moving his residence frequently, and never appeared in public alone.

Wilders was popular in the Netherlands but was never able to be part of a governing majority, because the other parties refused to work with him. Emblematic of the political establishment's reaction to the rise of "populists" such as Wilders was the fact that he has been tried several times for hatred and discrimination against Muslims. The first time, the charges were based on *Fitna*'s illustrations of how Islamic terror attacks were in line with passages of the Qur'an, and also on statements by Wilders criticizing Muhammad and Islam and comparing the Qur'an to *Mein Kampf*. In January 2009, the Amsterdam appeals court ordered the prosecution of Wilders for "inciting hatred and discrimination, based on comments by him in various media on Muslims and their beliefs. The court also considers appropriate criminal prosecution for insulting Muslim worshippers because of comparisons between Islam and Nazism made by Wilders."[446]

With an Orwellian twist, the court claimed that democracy itself mandated the prosecution of Wilders: "In a democratic system, hate speech is considered so serious that it is in the general interest to . . . draw a clear line."[447]

Wilders asserted, more accurately, that the prosecution was an "attack on the freedom of expression" and observed that "participation in the public debate has become a dangerous activity. If you give your opinion, you risk being prosecuted."[448]

Abdelmajid Khairoun, chairman of the Dutch Muslim Council (NMO), was happy with the prosecution, complaining that "Muslim youngsters who make anti-semitic remarks are prosecuted but Wilders' anti-Islamic remarks go unpunished."[449]

Wilders stated,

> People must know that I, a democratically elected politician who does not employ violence and the like, am being put on trial for speaking my mind and for making a movie (*Fitna*) that simply quotes the Koran itself. There must only be one outcome for this trial, and that is a full acquittal—and if not, Europe will pay a heavy price. . . . Many of our politicians in Europe are simply afraid; they are appeasers. . . . There is a lot of fear and a lot of political correctness, and the only way to deal with this is to stand up and not be afraid and not allow yourself to be intimidated.[450]

Wilders based his defense on the truthfulness of his words; he submitted a list of desired witnesses that included van Gogh's killer, Mohammed Bouyeri, as well as Britain-based jihad leader Anjem Choudary, Iranian Ayatollahs Ahmad Jannati and Mohammad Yazdi, Islamic scholar Hans Jansen, ex-Muslim Wafa Sultan, and this writer. The court disallowed most of these witnesses, frustrating Wilders's attempt to use his prosecution to place Islam and jihad on trial.[451]

Nonetheless, on June 23, 2011, Wilders was acquitted on all charges; Judge Marcel van Oosten appeared somewhat grudging about the verdict, calling Wilders's statements "gross and denigrating," but saying that they were "acceptable within the context of public debate."[452]

Wilders, describing himself as "incredibly happy," commented, "It's not only an acquittal for me, but a victory for freedom of expression in the Netherlands. Now the good news is that it's also legal to be critical about Islam, to speak publicly in a critical way about Islam and this is something that we need because the Islamisation of our societies is a major problem and a threat to our freedom and I'm allowed to say so."[453]

But the thought police were not through with Wilders. He was put on trial again in March 2016 for saying that there should not be more but fewer

Moroccans in the Netherlands. Prosecution spokeswoman Ilse de Heer asserted that this new prosecution of Wilders was different from the earlier one because this time Wilders had "targeted a specific race, which is considered a crime. . . . That is the difference now."[454]

Wilders was found guilty of "inciting discrimination."[455]

## Putting the elites on notice

In 2018, the British government imprisoned activist Tommy Robinson in what was widely seen as an attempt to silence and punish him for continuing to shed light on the Muslim rape gangs that all too many people in the country seemed determined to ignore. Robinson became something of a folk hero among Britons who rejected the elites' internationalism and commitment to mass migration, and on June 9, 2018, Wilders spoke at a massive rally for Robinson in London. Twenty thousand people came out to call for the activist's release, and Wilders took the opportunity to put the political elites of Britain and continental Europe on notice.

"Our governments," Wilders declared, "sold us out with mass immigration. With Islamization. With open borders. We are almost foreigners in our own lands. And if we complain about it, they call us racists and Islamophobes. But I say, no more! And what do you say? No more! And that's right: enough is enough. We will not be gagged anymore. No more tyranny."[456]

It was extraordinary that the British authorities allowed Wilders into the country at all. Several years before this, he was banned from entering the country, but although the ban was reversed on appeal, the British government in 2016 banned Martin Sellner, Brittany Pettibone, Lauren Southern, and Lutz Bachmann from entering, all for the crime of opposing jihad terror and Sharia oppression, and thereby made it clear that it is more authoritarian and unwilling to uphold the freedom of speech than ever—at least when it came to criticism of Islam, Muslim rape gangs, and mass Muslim migration. The banning of Sellner, Pettibone, Southern, and Bachmann was just part of a long pattern. Pamela Geller and I were banned from entering Britain in 2013, apparently for life, also for the crime of telling the truth about Islam and jihad.[457]

Yet at the same time, Britain had a steadily lengthening record of admitting jihad preachers without a moment of hesitation. Syed Muzaffar Shah Qadri's preaching of hatred and jihad violence was so hardline that he was banned from preaching in Pakistan, but the UK Home Office welcomed him into Britain.[458] The UK Home Office also admitted Shaykh Hamza Sodagar into the country, despite the fact that he had said, "If there's homosexual men, the punishment is one of five things. One—the easiest one maybe—chop their head off, that's the easiest. Second—burn them to death. Third—throw 'em off a cliff. Fourth—tear down a wall on them so they die under that. Fifth—a combination of the above."[459]

The British government likewise in 2016 admitted two jihad preachers who had praised the murderer of a foe of Pakistan's blasphemy laws.[460] One of them was welcomed by the Archbishop of Canterbury.[461] Meanwhile, the UK banned three bishops from areas of Iraq and Syria where Christians are persecuted from entering the country.[462]

By 2018, however, apparently British authorities decided that it would be too politically costly for them to bar Wilders again. And Wilders addressed them head-on, declaring, "We will not be silenced. We will not be intimidated. And we tell the governments, we are not afraid of you. We will never surrender. We will stand strong and do our duty. We will defend our civilization. And we will protect our people."[463]

Wilders added, "And I tell you, to the governments. You can throw us in jail, but you will never defeat us. Because, my friends, for every Tommy whom you imprison, thousands will rise up. So take notice, Theresa May. Take notice, Dutch Prime Minister Rutte. Take notice, Mrs. Merkel or President Macron. Take notice: the future is ours and not yours. We will defeat you politically, because we, my friends, we are the people."[464]

## France: Marine Le Pen

For many years, Wilders was one of the few voices in European politics to speak out against mass migration and Islamization. But as the situation worsened, other "populist" leaders eventually began to become prominent in several European countries.

In France, Marine Le Pen of the Rassemblement National (National Rally, or RN) was outspoken for years about the threat of mass migration, and for her pains was treated in much the same way as was Wilders in the Netherlands. Le Pen was accused in 2010 of "inciting discrimination, violence or hatred toward a group of people based on their religious beliefs" after she compared the de facto enforcement of Sharia law in areas of France to the German occupation during World War II: "If you want to talk about the occupation, let's talk about that, by the way, because here we are talking about the occupation of our space. It's an occupation of entire stretches of territory, of neighborhoods where religious law is applied. This is an occupation. Sure, there are no armored vehicles, no soldiers, but it's still an occupation, and it weighs on the inhabitants."[465]

For that, she faced a stiff fine and a jail term, but in December 2015, she was acquitted on the grounds that she hadn't meant to refer to all Muslims. The Collective Against Islamophobia in France, one of the groups that had filed complaints against Le Pen, groused, "This acquittal shows, once again, the legitimization and normalization of Islamophobia and of the hate speech that conveys it."[466] In reality, it was a rare victory—rare in contemporary Europe, that is—for the freedom of speech.

The elites were not finished. In September 2018, Le Pen was ordered by a French court to undergo a psychiatric examination in order to discover whether or not she was "capable of understanding remarks and answering questions."[467]

This doubt as to Le Pen's mental competence arose because she "tweeted out gruesome propaganda images from terror group Isis that showed the bodies of people having been executed by the so-called Islamic State."[468]

Le Pen, of course, did not tweet out these images out of a lurid fascination with blood and gore, or some secret sympathy for the Islamic State's jihad. She tweeted out those images because her party was being likened to the Islamic State in the French media. In a bid to bring the national discussion back to some semblance of sanity, she pointed out—by means of visual aids—that her party was not behaving in the same way as the Islamic State, and not leaving a trail of bloodshed and death in its wake.

But that meant nothing to the French authorities, who were desperate to destroy her, her movement, and any and all opposition to their globalist, socialist, open-borders agenda. She was charged with circulating "violent messages that incite terrorism or pornography or seriously harm human dignity." According to The Local, "as part of their investigation it appears magistrates in Nanterre near Paris have ordered Le Pen to visit a psychiatrist for an expert assessment."[469] Adding to the Orwellian flavor of the whole scenario was the fact that this order was issued on September 11.

Le Pen tried repeatedly to inject a note of sanity into this fantastically insane public discourse, stating, "I thought I had been through it all: well, no! For denouncing the horrors of Daesh (Isis) by tweets the 'justice system' has referred me for a psychiatric assessment. How far will they go?!"[470]

How far indeed? Le Pen is defiant: "Of course I will not go to this psychiatric assessment and I will wait to see how the magistrate intends to force me."[471] Le Pen also stated, "It's really incredible. This regime is really starting to worry me."[472] Understandably.

This all happened after Le Pen ran for president in 2017, losing to the globalist Emmanuel Macron. Her movement continued to grow, even after the claims that she could be mentally unbalanced; in the May 2019 elections for the European Parliament, the RN made substantial gains. Le Pen declared, "So it becomes a referendum for or against Emmanuel Macron, this European election. I accept that, but in these conditions, he must do as General De Gaulle: if he loses this election, then he will have to leave."[473] He did not, but there was no doubt that the pressure on him to act decisively to end the migrant influx and clean up the no-go zones had significantly increased.

French Prime Minister Edouard Philippe, another globalist, reacted to results relatively gracefully, but in a manner that made clear that Le Pen, like Wilders in the Netherlands, was still beyond acceptable limits for the political elites: "The far right is consolidating its positions," he said, using the media's favorite term of opprobrium for the populists; "this message is strong and we have received it. For my part, I welcome these results with humility. When we finish second, we can not say we won."[474] They did, however, continue to act as if they had.

## Hungary: Viktor Orban

In May 2010, Viktor Orban, who had served as Prime Minister of Hungary from 1998 to 2002, returned to that office. During the migrant crisis of 2015, Orban broke from EU policy by ordering a fence built on the Hungarian border with Serbia in order to keep the migrants out of his country. Orban also initiated a number of other measures that Hungary took in order to prevent the country from being inundated by migrants.

While in Romania on a state visit in July 2017, Orban accused George Soros, the billionaire who has funded innumerable internationalist, socialist causes, of working by means of the European Union to create a "new, mixed, Muslimized Europe."[475] Orban declared that "the European Union, the European Commission must regain independence from the Soros Empire before the billionaire finishes his program for the destruction of the continent."[476]

Predictably, this kind of talk earned Orban the undying ire of the European elites. In September 2018, the European Parliament's Sargentini Report accused the Hungarian government of various violations of human rights, leading to an attempt to place economic sanctions upon the country. In response, the Orban government released a video depicting the European Parliament's Guy Verhofstadt, a strong proponent of a politically united Europe and a vociferous foe of nationalism and populism. "This is Guy Verhofstadt," the video began. "He wants more migration."[477] Verhofstadt was then pictured saying, "We need migration."[478]

The Hungarian government's video then stated, "These are the facts: 1.8 million migrants have entered the European Union since 2015. Millions more wish to come. Since the crisis began hundreds have lost their lives in vicious attacks all across Europe. Violent crime is rising. And Guy Verhofstadt wants more migration. This is reckless. Time to shake up Brussels. Let's protect Europe!"[479]

In line with this, Orban's response to the migrant influx was simple and direct, and starkly different from that of Western European countries. In response to threats from Erdogan of a new migrant inundation, Orban warned in October 2019 that "if Turkey sets off further hundreds of thousands (on top of those it has already), then we will need to use force to protect the Hungarian border and the Serbian–Hungarian frontier and I do not wish for anyone that we should need to resort to that."[480]

Orban added, "The next weeks will decide what Turkey does with these people.... It can steer them in two directions: take them back to Syria or set them off towards Europe. If Turkey chooses the latter, these people will arrive at Hungary's southern border in huge masses."[481] Instead, they were stopped at the Greek border, at least for the time being.

## Italy: Matteo Salvini

Hungary's Orban said that he was a "great admirer" of Matteo Salvini, who served as Italy's Deputy Prime Minister and Minister of the Interior from June 1, 2018, to September 5, 2019, and added, "He is my hero, a companion of my destiny."[482] In light of Italy's de facto role as the entry point for many migrants into Europe, Orban said in August 2018, "The security of the European Union depends on Salvini's success and we urge him not to flinch" in his opposition to mass migration.[483] Hungary, said Orban, would offer Italy "all our help" to protect its borders.[484]

"We are close," said Orban, "to a historic turning point for the future of Europe: today a journey of meetings begins, there will be many others."[485] The journey, he said, was on the way to creating "a different Europe" that "puts the right to work, health, and security in the center."[486]

Salvini did not flinch. While he was deputy prime minister and interior minister in April 2019, he attempted to move toward the same goal. Referring to a notorious incident in which a Muslim migrant stabbed a man who was wearing a crucifix necklace on a bus in Rome, Salvini said, "Rome does not deserve certain scenes," and called for heightened security as well as immigration control.[487]

Salvini also took aim at Islamic centers, some of which were breeding grounds for jihad terror activity: "According to the data of the updated census of Islamic presences in Italy to date there are 1,382 Islamic cultural associations, of which 1,068 are also used as a place for prayer. Obviously it is full of good people but there are also realities underlined by the police to identify the presence of fanatics and extremists."[488] He called for the monitoring of mosques and Islamic cultural centers.

Salvini, however, was not able to navigate successfully the always turbulent waters of Italian politics. Although he lost his positions in the Italian government in 2019, he is still a force in Italian politics. And of course, words he spoke in August 2018 remain true: "At this point the left exists only to insult me and defend a banker-led EU and boundless immigration." He praised Orban's success, which he clearly wanted to replicate: "In Hungary, unemployment is under 5 percent, the flat tax for business is at 9 percent and at 15 percent for individuals, immigration is under control, and the economy has been growing at 4 percent."[489] He may still get a chance to do so.

## Denouncing populism

There were other populist movements in Europe as well: the Sweden Democrats, the Alliance for Germany, and others. The Brexit movement to separate Britain from the European Union was motivated in large part by a desire to free the nation from the European Union's requirements regarding mass migration. As these movements were growing, however, the European political elites themselves grew all the more determined to crush populism once and for all. In September 2018, European Union official Pierre Moscovici called for "more progress in European integration" in order to destroy populism, which he claimed was "a major threat for our democracies, for liberal democracies, for the rule of law and for European values."[490]

Demonstrating that he had no idea of the deep discontent in Europe over mass migration, no-go zones, rising crime, and the destruction of the freedom of speech, Moscovici, a former member of France's Revolutionary Communist League, ascribed the rise of populism to a failure on the part of European authorities to "deliver," saying, "The European crisis is no more an economic crisis. It is an inequality crisis. It is a political crisis. It is a crisis of delivery. We need to deliver more. That is what eurozone reform is about. It is not technical. It is highly political."[491] The eurozone was designed to bring an end to national sovereignty over economics and finance.

There were economic and political aspects to the crisis, but Moscovici betrayed no awareness of the tremendous cultural and societal upheaval that the policies he supported had brought about.

Neither did European Commission President Jean-Claude Juncker, who in September 2016 warned that Europe must be prevented from "going down the path of nationalization," and claimed that what the continent needed was more "union."[492] In October 2018, Juncker attacked "stupid populists," although at the same time he admitted that there were legitimate "Eurosceptics who have questions to ask and opinions to make."[493] Juncker acknowledged that "in Europe, there is an increasing number of Eurosceptics and they tend to be promoting Eurosceptical opinions."[494] He said magnanimously, "We should talk to them," while adding a caveat that showed that such talks would be pointless: "We cannot build Europe against the nations and the regions."[495]

Pope Francis, an indefatigable supporter of mass migration, no doubt would have agreed. In January 2017, he warned that with the rise of populism, "there is a risk of history repeating itself."[496] He had the Nazis in mind: "For me the most typical example of populism in the European sense is the Germany of 1933."[497] After Hindenburg, said the Pope, "Germany tries to get back up, searches for its identity, looks for a leader, someone to give it back its identity and a youngster named Adolf Hitler says, 'I can do it; I can do it.'"[498]

The Pope accused populists of preying upon "people's fears" with "a message of hate."[499] He cautioned against the impulse to "look for a savior who gives us back our identity and let's defend ourselves with walls, barbed-wire, whatever, from other people that may rob us of our identity."[500]

In October 2018 Pope Francis once again denounced populism in furious language, returning to his suggestion that its proponents were essentially Europe's new Nazis: "It is important for young people to know how populism is born. I think of Hitler in the last century, who had promised development for Germany. They should know how populisms begin: by sowing hate. You can't live sowing hate."[501] The Pope did not, on this or any other occasion, explain why opposing mass migration was "sowing hate," rather than showing a rational and justified concern for the safety and wellbeing of one's family and society.

"Study your history," the Pope added; "this is the way the Führer started, with racial purity."[502] He did not, of course, explain why the populist forces so frequently described as racist and xenophobic actually had no problem at all with migrant groups that showed a readiness to assimilate and accept the values of their new land. As far as Francis was concerned, the entire controversy about mass migration was about hate: "We are now in full World War III fought piecemeal and even religion is deformed to be able to hate better."[503]

The Pontiff warned, "Making hatred grow, creating violence and division represents a path to destruction and suicide."[504] He also reiterated a point he had made many times, that acquiescing to mass migration was not just a matter of accepting a certain aspect of public policy but a moral imperative. The migrants, he declared, "must be welcomed with an open heart and open doors. Closure is the path to suicide. It is true that migrants must be welcomed, but they must also be accompanied and above all they must be integrated. A government must have an open heart to receive and good structures to assist integration, and also the prudence to say: I can do it up to this point, but no further."[505] Appealing to the residual Christian conscience of post-Christian Europe, the Pope also said that welcoming the migrants was "a biblical mandate. We think of Europe that has been made by migrants, by cultures mixing together."[506]

Just before the European Parliament elections in May 2019, Germany's Merkel, speaking in Zagreb, warned: "There are populist currents that in many areas disdain these values," that is, the European Union's support for internationalism and mass migration, "that want to destroy our European values."[507] She added: "Nationalism is the enemy of the European project, and we have to make that clear in the last days before the election."[508] That European project, she claimed, was a "project of peace," a "project of freedom," and a "project of prosperity."[509]

Merkel insisted that "our values mean we can be proud of our own country and at the same time work to build Europe."[510]

=Manfred Weber of Merkel's Christian Democratic Union (CDU) reiterated his government's determination not to work with populists after the election, just as the Dutch mainstream parties had shunned Geert Wilders for years: "Right-wing populists and extremists are those who want to destroy Europe, who are not believing any more in partnership on this continent, and we will fight against them."[511]

## *"Hungarians gave us the task of . . . stopping immigration all across Europe"*

In many areas, however, the tide was going against the globalists and internationalists. Hungary, Poland, and other Central and Eastern European nations refused to take the migrant influx and stood up to the European Union's demands that they open their borders.

In Hungarian elections in April 2018, Viktor Orban was re-elected and told supporters, "We have won, Hungary has won a great victory. There is a big battle behind us, we have won a crucial victory, giving ourselves a chance to defend Hungary."[512]

Orban had more than the defense of Hungary in mind. In the European Parliamentary elections in May 2019, his Fidesz Party won a decisive victory. Orban asserted that the results were significant far beyond the borders of Hungary itself. "The election victory," he said to a cheering crowd in Budapest, "means that . . . Hungarians gave us the task of . . . stopping immigration all across Europe."[513] Hungarians, he declared, wanted Fidesz to "protect Christian culture in Europe."[514]

Martin Helme, the leader of the Estonian Conservative People's Party (EKRE) and, after the May 2019 elections, Estonia's Minister of Finance, also shared Orban's distaste for the EU's mass migration policies, and for the European Union itself. When asked if he supported Estonia's becoming more integrated into the EU, Helme replied, "I don't see a reason for 'ever closer union' and I don't support deeper integration in the EU in general. We should first do what we have agreed and not focus on finding new ways of integration or deepening integration."[515]

France's Emmanuel Macron was having none of this. In September 2018, he vowed action against European countries that rejected the migrant influx. "Europe is not a menu à la carte, it's a political project," he stated, and he blamed countries that "refuse to let boats on [their] ports" for the "crisis and tensions" within the European Union.[516] Macron singled out the Visegrad nations, the Czech Republic, Hungary, Poland, and Slovakia, for special criticism for their refusal to accept the migrants. Macron attacked "the leaders who tell me . . . '[I] love Europe when it gives me money, when it makes my people prosperous, when it allows my workers to make better a living in neighbouring countries,' but at home, will not take a single migrant, not a single refugee."[517] He threatened to cut off this money flow: "Countries that do not want more Frontex [the European Union's border agency] or solidarity [in housing and feeding third world migrants] will leave Schengen. Countries that don't want more Europe will no longer [get access to] structural funds."[518]

Orban was not intimidated. In March 2020, as the Turkish government abetted migrants attacking Greek forces blocking them from entering the European Union countries, the Hungarian Prime Minister said that the EU should "give all the help we can" to Greece to stop the migrants, adding, "It won't be enough just to defend the Greek–Turkish border."[519]

At a summit with other Visegrad Group leaders, Orban said, "As a last resort, as in 2015, there are the Hungarians. Even if Greece's attempt [to keep the migrants out] is successful, the EU border must be defended . . . which Hungary will do."[520]

# CHAPTER 8

## THE FUTURE OF EUROPE

### *European or Muslim?*

The Muslims of Europe and America today appear to be caught between two worlds and betray a marked ambivalence about which one they will ultimately choose. A crucial element of that choice involves the question of individual identity. Is a European or American Muslim primarily a European or an American, or a Muslim?

Two Americans—Muhammad Junaid and Sergeant Hasan Akbar—highlight the difficulty of this choice. Akbar was an American serviceman who attacked his fellow American soldiers with grenades while shouting about the threat they posed to "our countries." Junaid said he was an American computer programmer in New York whose mother had survived the World Trade Center attacks—whereupon Junaid traveled to Afghanistan to fight with the Taliban. Junaid's story could not be verified, and he may have fabricated every bit of it except for his presence in Afghanistan, where he was interviewed; but the one part of it that rings true was his statement that "I may hold an American passport, but I am not an American, I am a Muslim."[521]

Echoes of the same idea, that Islam transcends all nationality and particularly nationality in a non-Muslim country, abound in the writings of numerous Muslim radicals—notably the influential Egyptian thinker Sayyid Qutb (1906–1966), a key intellectual forerunner of modern-day Muslim terrorists. Qutb revived and insisted upon the sharp division first drawn by medieval Muslim divines between the Muslim world and the world of unbelief:

> There is only one place on earth which can be called the home of Islam (Dar-ul-Islam), and it is that place where the Islamic state is established and the Shari'ah is the authority and God's limits are observed, and where all the Muslims administer the affairs of the state with mutual consultation. The rest of the world is the home of hostility (Dar-ul-Harb). A Muslim can have only two possible relations with Dar-ul-Harb: peace with a contractual agreement, or

107

war. A country with which there is a treaty will not be considered the home of Islam.[522]

Consequently, he argued that a Muslim cannot be in the full sense a citizen of a non-Muslim state, and that even his status as a citizen of a Muslim state is secondary to his status as a Muslim:

> A Muslim has no country except that part of the earth where the Shari'ah of God is established and human relationships are based on the foundation of relationship with God; a Muslim has no nationality except his belief, which makes him a member of the Muslim community in Dar-ul-Islam; a Muslim has no relatives except those who share the belief in God, and thus a bond is established between him and other Believers through their relationship with God.[523]

## The duplicity of Tariq Ramadan

While Qutb's ideas still have wide currency among Muslims around the world, other Muslims in Europe have sounded different notes. One Muslim in France, Kamel Hamza, articulated the opposite of Qutb's position, saying: "I'm French first, but also Algerian."[524] And for a considerable period, the Muslim thinker Tariq Ramadan enjoyed wide popularity, in large part for the guidance he offered on how to sort out the competing demands of Islam and secularism.

Ramadan, who is now awaiting trial on multiple rape charges in France, is the author of a book entitled *To Be a European Muslim*, in which he called for the discarding of the traditional Islamic division of the world into the *dar al-Islam* (House of Islam) and the *dar al-Harb* (House of War). Ramadan instead suggested that Muslims see Europe as *"dar ash-shahada"*—House of Testimony.[525] (The Shahada is the Muslim confession of faith: "There is no god but Allah and Muhammad is His Prophet.") This would involve bearing witness to their faith through words and deeds; an essential element of doing this, Ramadan insisted, would be to obey the laws of European society, in which Muslims found themselves. *"Implementing the Shari'a*, for a Muslim citizen or resident in Europe," he says, "is explicitly to respect the constitutional and legal framework of the country in which he is a citizen"[526] (italics in original). Very well, but what would this mean for the day when a Western European country has a Muslim majority? Would Ramadan and his followers then call for the implementation of Sharia in full?

One clue to the answer to that question may lie in the fact that Ramadan has rejected the cardinal principle of Islamic radicalism, which is that the Sharia is the only valid law. "Today," Ramadan stated, "I think that Islam is completely compatible with the separation of the Church and the State."[527] A contrary clue, however, may be found in how Ramadan has reacted to the rape charges against him. In December 2019, he acknowledged some nebulous wrongdoing, but then claimed that the accusations against him were all an attempt to discredit him, and thereby to "neutralize the Muslims."[528] This was a manifestation of the same victimhood paranoia we see so often from Sharia supremacists in Europe and elsewhere whenever they're accused of any wrongdoing at all.

"We have to be clear," Ramadan said, "that there is discrimination, stigmatization, racism that is at stake in the whole issue."[529] He continued: "And I was a symbol. To destroy me meant, let the people understand: If you want to be vocal you have to face the reality. It happened to Tariq Ramadan now, it could happen to anyone in the future."[530]

Even worse, RFI reported in February 2020 that "the prominent Islamic scholar Tariq Ramadan has been formally charged with raping two more women, adding to two existing charges of rape. The charges were pronounced on Thursday at the end of a court hearing in Paris.... Supporters of Ramadan, who is a professor of contemporary Islamic studies at Oxford's St. Anthony's College, have called the accusations against him part of a 'international Zionist plot' to blacken his name."[531]

A Zionist plot. An alternative view was that a cosseted Muslim academic, hailed and feted all over Europe and the United States, began to indulge his worst impulses, tempted to do so when it became clear that, in light of his value to Western authorities as a "moderate Muslim" who seemed to prop up their fantasies about the jihad threat, he would be allowed to get away with virtually anything.

"Virtually anything" was actually an understatement. The allegations against Ramadan were particularly revolting; if they are true, he was a monstrous sadist. One of his accusers said he subjected her to "blows to the face and body, forced sodomy, rape with an object and various humiliations, including being dragged by the hair to the bathtub and urinated on."[532] His sadism appeared to be, if the allegations were true, closely intertwined with his celebrated Islamic piety: another one of his accusers said he told her he was raping her because she didn't wear a hijab.[533]

He would have gotten away with it all, being just too valuable for the Western political and media elites, if it hadn't been for the #MeToo movement. Even now, it wouldn't be at all surprising, given his connections to all varieties of powerful people, if Ramadan were cleared of all the charges. If this happens, it would be in keeping with the duplicity that has characterized his entire career. French journalist Caroline Fourest's illuminating book *Brother Tariq: The Doublespeak of Tariq Ramadan* concluded Ramadan was actually anything but a reformer: in reality, she wrote, Ramadan was "remaining scrupulously faithful to the strategy mapped out by his grandfather, a strategy of advance stage by stage" toward the imposition of Islamic law in the West.[534]

Ramadan, she explained, in his public lectures and writings invests words like "law" and "democracy" with subtle and carefully crafted new definitions, permitting him to engage in "an apparently inoffensive discourse while remaining faithful to an eminently Islamist message and without having to lie overtly—at least not in his eyes."[535] Far from being an actual Islamic reformer whose teachings would help young Muslims in Europe become Europeans, Ramadan, she said, "may have an influence on young Islamists and constitute a factor of incitement that could lead them to join the partisans of violence."[536]

Fourest was the first to reveal, back in 2017, long before these new charges were levied, that Ramadan had at least four other victims besides the first woman who came forward, Henda Ayari. "A request for religious advice turned into a compulsive sexual relationship, sometimes consented to, often violent and very humiliating, before ending in threats."[537] Fourest had evidence. "I presented it to a judge. But Tariq Ramadan scared him too much. ... I am well-placed to know the violence of the networks of the Muslim Brotherhood when one stands up to 'brother Tariq.'"[538]

A judge being scared of Tariq Ramadan was eminently believable. For appearing to dispute venerable elements of Islamic tradition publicly and offering a version of Islam that appears to be harmonious with Western secularism, Ramadan had become a media darling. In February 2002, Paul Donnelly of *Salon* magazine anointed Ramadan the "Muslim Martin Luther."[539]

Ramadan vigilantly guarded his reputation as a moderate. When the French *Lyon* magazine suggested that he had secret pro-jihad sentiments, calling him "the king of ambiguity," "seemingly inoffensive," and "a veritable time bomb," he sued.[540]

Still, even before the allegations of sexual assault, Ramadan was not exactly what his Western boosters would have liked him to be. Many of his statements seemed studiedly ambiguous. He admitted the possibility that "a Muslim is allowed to live in a non-Islamic country" only so long as he was "able to protect his identity and practice his religion."[541] In 1999, he reminded Muslims that "there exists a general Islamic ruling which forbids a Muslim to fight or kill a fellow Muslim and this ruling should be observed at all times. Therefore, a Muslim citizen of a Western country, in order to avoid placing himself in such a situation, should also plead conscientious objection."[542] U.S. Army Major Nidal Malik Hasan offered exactly that defense for murdering 13 Americans at Fort Hood in 2009.

Referring to Islamic law's death sentence for apostates, Ramadan argued that it didn't apply to "one who would leave the faith for personal conviction without trying to betray Islam and Muslims thereafter, in any way."[543] He added: "The necessary attitude is therefore a minimal respect for the faith that one leaves and a sensitivity by those that continue to practice it."[544] Ramadan didn't explain what form this "minimal respect" must take, and since he left the death penalty in place for those who do dared to "betray Islam and Muslims" thereafter, one may legitimately wonder just how compatible his self-proclaimed moderate vision of Islam really is with European secularism.

Ramadan is the grandson of Hasan al-Banna (1906–1949), the founder of the pioneering modern Islamic extremist group, Egypt's Muslim Brotherhood. He has said that he rejects certain aspects of his radical grandfather's teachings:

> Clearly there is a difference between what [al-Banna] said in his day and what I am saying today. I am living and speaking out more than 50 years after he was assassinated, that is, in a different era and in a different historical context. Over the years there have been various developments that I am taking into account in formulating my positions, positions that are congruent with my principles. There are some things of my grandfather's with which I agree and others with which I don't agree.[545]

Nevertheless, Ramadan contributed a foreword to an edition of Hasan al-Banna's *Risalat al-Ma'thurat,* a collection by al-Banna of key texts from the Qur'an and the Hadith, the traditions of the Prophet Muhammad. Ramadan describes the book as "the core of spiritual education for all members of the

Muslim Brotherhood."[546] He wrote glowingly of his grandfather, lauding al-Banna for the "quality of his faith and the intensity of his relationship with God. Anyone who had ever been in contact with him perceived and experienced this." He describes al-Banna's teachings as "simple and luminous."[547]

In this document at least, he gave no hint that he rejected any of al-Banna's thought. Yet his unreserved praise was hard to reconcile with his carefully cultivated image as a Muslim reformer. Readers of this foreword may have been forgiven for getting the impression that Ramadan was labeling "simple and luminous" such aspects of al-Banna's thought as his insistence that Muslims must make war against Jews and Christians. "In [Muslim] Tradition," al-Banna writes, "there is a clear indication of the obligation to fight the People of the Book [that is, Jews and Christians], and of the fact that God doubles the reward of those who fight them. Jihad is not against polytheists alone, but against all who do not embrace Islam."[548]

In his depiction of a downtrodden Muslim world invaded by the West and with jihad as its only recourse, Al-Banna sounded like many jihad leaders today:

> Today the Muslims, as you know, are compelled to humble themselves before non-Muslims, and are ruled by unbelievers. Their lands have been trampled over, and their honor besmirched. Their adversaries are in charge of their affairs, and the rites of their religion have fallen into abeyance within their own domains, to say nothing of their impotence to broadcast the summons [to embrace Islam]. Hence it has become an individual obligation, which there is no evading, on every Muslim to prepare his equipment, to make up his mind to engage in jihad, and to get ready for it until the opportunity is ripe and God decrees a matter which is sure to be accomplished.[549]

Did he mean a military jihad? Most certainly: "Know then that death is inevitable, and that it can only happen once. If you suffer it in the way of God, it will be your profit in this world, and your reward in the next."[550]

Most telling of all may be the fact that Tariq Ramadan, by his own account, based his famous objection to the *dar al-harb* designation on the grounds that it "does not derive from the Quur'ân, and is not part of the Prophetic tradition."[551] Ramadan declares that "Muslims must take from the West those values that do not contradict Islam," but he never directly calls upon Muslims to discard elements of the Qur'an and Islamic law that contradict the principles of secular society. As a citizen of Switzerland, he warns, "Don't ask me to be a less Muslim to be a good Swiss."[552]

Consequently, it is hard to see how any reform his teachings might inspire could escape the assessment of the Muslim writer A. L. Tibawi: "Perceptible 'reform' cannot be affected in the doctrines of the faith without diminishing or cancelling their validity."[553] Yet among the doctrines of the faith are teachings about armed jihad and the subjugation of non-Muslims—teachings that are strongly reaffirmed by Muslim radicals such as Ramadan's grandfather.

Al-Banna's teachings, whatever Ramadan really thinks of them, are still influential enough among Muslims in Europe and elsewhere to be reprinted in handsome new editions complete with words of praise from the author's famous grandson.

As long as Muslims in Europe and around the world continue to value these writings, the specter of jihad and Sharia is not likely to disappear from Europe or anywhere else anytime soon.

## *The future according to the Islamic State*

### The ISIS Hijrah

An Islamic State operative boasted in September 2015 that among the flood of refugees, 4,000 Islamic State jihadis had already entered Europe. He explained their purpose: "It's our dream that there should be a caliphate not only in Syria but in all the world, and we will have it soon, inshallah."[554] These Muslims were going to Europe in the service of that caliphate: "They are going like refugees," he said, but they were going with the plan of sowing blood and mayhem on European streets.[555] As he told this to journalists, he smiled and said, "Just wait."[556] We are waiting in the U.S. as well.

Hijrah, or emigration for the purpose of Islamization, according to Islamic tradition has its primary model in the migration or journey of Muhammad and his followers from Mecca to Yathrib, later renamed by him to Medina, in the year 622 CE. It was after the Hijrah that Muhammad for the first time became not just a preacher of religious ideas, but a political and military leader. That was what occasioned his new "revelations" exhorting his followers to commit violence against unbelievers. Significantly, the Islamic calendar counts the Hijrah, not Muhammad's birth or the occasion of his first "revelation," as the beginning of Islam, implying that Islam is not fully itself without a political and military component.

To emigrate in the cause of Allah—that is, to move to a new land in order to bring Islam there, is considered in Islam to be a highly meritorious act. "And whoever emigrates for the cause of Allah will find on the earth many locations and abundance," says the Qur'an. "And whoever leaves his home as an emigrant to Allah and His Messenger and then death overtakes him, his reward has already become incumbent upon Allah. And Allah is ever Forgiving and Merciful" (4:100). The exalted status of such emigrants led a British jihad group that won notoriety (and a shutdown by the government) a few years ago for celebrating 9/11 to call itself Al-Muhajiroun: The Emigrants.

National Intelligence Director James Clapper acknowledged in April 2016 that "we continue to see evidence" of Islamic State activity all over Europe. He added: "We've learned that they are fanatic, very operational security conscious—they're very mindful of that. They have taken advantage to some extent of the migrant crisis in Europe."[557]

## Conquering Rome

While Rome protected itself from Oriana Fallaci, the Islamic invaders and their allies made their plans for the city plain. Sheik Ali Al-Faqir, former Jordanian minister of religious endowment, said on Al-Aqsa TV on May 2, 2008, "We proclaim that we will conquer Rome, like Constantinople was conquered once."[558] Hamas MP and Islamic cleric Yunis Al-Astal said, also on Al-Aqsa TV, on April 11, 2008, "Very soon, Allah willing, Rome will be conquered, just like Constantinople was, as was prophesized by our Prophet Muhammad."[559] In May 2014, a Kosovar Muslim in Iraq said, "We shall conquer Jerusalem from you, O Jews! We shall conquer Rome and Andalusia, Allah willing."[560]

In a Friday sermon in February 2016, Edmonton, Alberta, imam Sheikh Shaban Sherif Mady declared, "'Constantinople will be conquered.' It is the Prophet Muhammad who said so. And what was Constantinople? Just like the Vatican today, it was the capital of all the Christians in the world. It was conquered and became Turkey. The Hagia Sophia became a great mosque, where Allah is worshipped. The prophecies of the Prophet Muhammad came true. But some prophecies have not come true yet. Look forward to it, because the Prophet Muhammad said that Rome would be conquered! It will be conquered. Constantinople was conquered. Rome is the Vatican, the very heart of the Christian state."[561]

Sheikh Yusuf al-Qaradawi, the most prominent and renowned imam in the world, in writing about "signs of the victory of Islam," referred to the same hadith:

> The Prophet Muhammad was asked: "What city will be conquered first, Constantinople or Romiyya?" He answered: "The city of Hirqil [i.e., the Byzantine emperor Heraclius] will be conquered first"— that is, Constantinople; Romiyya is the city today called "Rome," the capital of Italy. The city of Hirqil [that is, Constantinople] was conquered by the young 23-year-old Ottoman Muhammad bin Morad, known in history as Muhammad the Conqueror, in 1453. The other city, Romiyya, remains, and we hope and believe [that it too will be conquered]. This means that Islam will return to Europe as a conqueror and victor, after being expelled from it twice—once from the South, from Andalusia, and a second time from the East, when it knocked several times on the door of Athens.[562]

Another hadith depicts Muhammad as saying, "You will attack Arabia and Allah will enable you to conquer it, then you would attack Persia and He would make you to conquer it. Then you would attack Rome and Allah will enable you to conquer it, then you would attack the Dajjal and Allah will enable you to conquer him. Nafi' said, Jabir, we thought that the Dajjal would appear after Rome would be conquered."[563] The Dajjal is an evil figure of Islamic eschatology; his appearance after the Muslim conquest of Rome would herald the end of the world and the consummation of all things.

This prophecy is quite important to the Islamic State (ISIS). In a lengthy threat to the West issued on September 21, 2014, an Islamic State spokesman boasted, "We will conquer your Rome, break your crosses, and enslave your women, by the permission of Allah, the Exalted. This is His promise to us; He is glorified and He does not fail in His promise. If we do not reach that time, then our children and grandchildren will reach it, and they will sell your sons as slaves at the slave market."[564] The Washington Post reported in February 2015 that "in a recently released video that showed the killing of 21 Christians in Libya, all but one of them Egyptian, the Islamic State issued an ominous warning: 'Today we are south of Rome,' one masked militant said. 'We will conquer Rome with Allah's permission.'"[565]

Yet despite all this and much more that makes clear the Islamic aspiration to conquer Rome, Oriana Fallaci's observation that "the Islamic invasion does not proceed only in a physical sense, but also in a mental and cultural sense" also had abundant attestation. After Islamic jihadists murdered over 130 people in Paris in November 2015, Rome's Prefect Franco Gabrielli said characterized the massacre as "an attack by criminals and the first victims are Muslims themselves."[566] Gabrielli no doubt considered Oriana Fallaci to have been an "Islamophobe."

## The jihad against Europe

Not just Rome is in the sights of those who wish to conquer. On April 12, 2020, Easter Sunday, members of the Vejleå Church in Ishøj, Denmark found that a wall of their church had been painted with the phrases "We conquer Denmark" and "There is no God but Allah."[567] The graffiti was in Arabic.

The graffiti artists may have been making empty boasts, but others were not. Early in 2015, the Islamic State, which has lost its domains in Iraq and Syria but is by no means dead, released an e-book entitled *Black Flags from Rome* as part of its series detailing its plans for world conquest. Other titles in the series included *Black Flags from the East, Black Flags from Syria, Black Flags from Arabia*, and *Black Flags from Persia*.

All of these detail why and how the various areas specified can and must be conquered. *Black Flags from the East, Black Flags from Syria, Black Flags from Arabia*, and *Black Flags from Persia* detail the Islamic State's plans for the conquest of the Muslim areas outside its domains, with particular emphasis on two of its most formidable foes, Saudi Arabia and Iran. *Black Flags from Rome* explains how this jihad would also be extended into non-Muslim domains, Europe in particular.

*Black Flags from Rome* begins with a quotation from the Qur'an that sets the tone for the whole thing (material in parentheses and brackets as written by the Islamic State): "And I (Allah [God]) wanted to do a favour to those who were weak and oppressed in the land, and to make them rulers" (Quran 28:5).[568]

## Borrowing leftist fantasies: The rise of "far-right racist groups"

The theme of the whole piece is that the Muslims in Europe are "weak and oppressed," and that they can and must rise up against non-Muslim Europeans and conquer Rome and Europe for Islam.

To portray Muslims in Europe as oppressed, *Black Flags from Rome* paints a paranoid and contrary-to-reality picture of a European continent full of "armed gangs" that are "forming into militias for racist politicians" and "far-right racist groups" being "funded by racist rich people."[569]

These racists are—for reasons unexplained—focused in particular upon Islam. These groups started off "as people who were against immigration," but soon "their leaders were paid to oppose Islam especially."[570]

> Europe is returning to the Dark Ages [due to the financial recession]. Armed gangs are forming into militias for racist politicians, and a young Muslim minority is their enemy. All this while a Caliphate is growing across the Mediterranean sea next door.[571]

The idea that European governments were behind these groups was ridiculous, as the European political establishment viciously hounded groups that were opposed to Islamization—but as far as the Islamic State was concerned, all this is coming to a head and leading to the conquest of Rome.

## Increasingly assertive and aggressive Muslim populations

The document offers a history of Muslim immigration into Europe, identifying three waves of. The first immigrant generation "was satisfied with a basic living" and "did not want to offend their European rulers and felt grateful to them for giving them a job, a home to live in and a mosque to pray at in their European land." They were grateful for these things because they hadn't had them back home, and that, too, was the Europeans' fault: "They had been prevented from these basic human rights in their homelands by the puppet rulers (which the colonisers had put on thrones before they left). So these immigrants were grateful for even a little."

The second generation, which the Islamic State places as between 1960 and 1980, was focused on ensuring that "their families were rich and had high ranking jobs so they support the poorer family members 'back home.'"[572] The third generation, thriving now, would be different: "Unlike their parents version of Islam, which was more cultural and subservient, this

117

new generation, would start studying the life of Allah (God's) Messenger, Muhammad (peace be on him) and comparing it to their situation in Europe."

As a result of these studies, this generation

> had given up the victim subservient slave mentality the previous generations had. This generation would be emboldened and more confident in their newly (re)discovered beliefs. They would see the world from a new perspective, and unlike the previous generations who only dedicated on earning money for supporting the family "back home", this new generation would see the world through the eyes of a global Ummah (Muslim nation) which transcended all national boundaries.[573]

The Islamic State's e-book doesn't say it, but aiding and abetting this generational development was the European embrace of multiculturalism, which led to the earlier idea that immigrants must be assimilated being rejected as "racist" and "ethnocentric." Immigrants into Europe (and the United States as well) were encouraged to keep and celebrate their own cultures and traditions rather than embrace those of their new home—an idea that played right into the hands of those who believed that all earthly loyalties must take second place to the believers' adherence to the "global Ummah" that "transcended all national boundaries."

## Smuggling lessons

Meanwhile, "Many Jihad preachers and supporters who left Afghanistan came to Europe as refugees in the early 90s, and later married convert Muslim women and got permanent stay where they lived. Countries with the biggest Jihadi populations in Europe were; Belgium, France, and later the UK."[574] These preachers took advantage of lax and conflicting laws in European countries:

> The Jihad preachers and supporters in the West took advantage of the different laws within each country. In the early 90s, many went to Belgium (located: North of France) due to its relaxed laws against supporting armed groups. However, once the Belgium government found out there were many Jihadis' there, it made stricter laws against them so many fled to the UK where the laws were also soft (this would change in the 2000s). France has a huge Muslim Arab population, and they knew that many Arab Jihadis' from the GIA

were in their country. They would try to arrest them but many of the leaders who inspired the youth were in the UK. But the UK would not hand the preachers over to France because the preachers had not broken any laws in the UK. This caused the European intelligence agencies to be bitter against each other in the early to mid-90s.[575]

The GIA was the Armed Islamic Group, a jihad group in Algeria. *Black Flags from Rome* offers a fascinating glimpse into how such groups operated in Europe as jihadis smuggled weapons from there into Algeria:

> They would receive donations from supporters in Europe and with them donations buy weapons for the GIA. From where? From Europe, and transport them into the Islamic Maghrib. They would buy the weapons and then take them to a car mechanic who worked for them, who would dismantle the car and place the cash and weapons inside the cars (deep in the interior framework) and fix the car back together again. These cars would then be driven by GIA members pretending to be natives going on a holiday from France to Spain, and from Spain by Ferry (ship) to Morocco, and from Morocco into Algeria. A middle-person would then collect the car in Morocco and take it to the location of the fighters who would receive the car, dismantle it and extract what was inside. This is how they smuggled weapons from France to Algeria.[576]

This wasn't just anecdotal history, this was strategizing for the next jihad: "No doubt, if a war in Europe is to spark in the future, this whole process will be reversed and weapons will be smuggled in a similar way from the Islamic Maghrib into the heart of Europe."[577]

## "Extremists" and "moderates"

The other side, according to *Black Flags from Rome*, was mobilizing as well: "In 1998, the New World Order was beginning to take place, and European countries began to work together in fighting against Islam."[578] And after 9/11, "the Western intelligence agencies began to change their laws and co-operate together to capture and lock up the preachers who were the most outspoken within the 90s. Groups and organisations made by the preachers were closed down and banned. Spies and listening devices were installed in the Muslim mosques and community centres everywhere."[579] But the

Western officials' task was difficult, as "many AQ [al-Qaeda] members captured in Muslim lands had shaven their beards for deception and hiding their devout Muslim identity."[580]

*Black Flags from Rome* remarks upon the absurdity of Western authorities' inability or unwillingness to deal with the ideological roots of the challenge they were facing:

> The Western policy makers had to play a powerful balancing act. They would fight the Muslim world while trying to stop Muslims from becoming 'radicalised' and reactionary violent. This was almost impossible, so they came up with a clever plan. They would begin to divide Muslims in the media as 'extremists' (who supported Jihad) and 'moderates.' (those who didn't).[581]

The Islamic State rejected the distinction, preferring one between those Muslims whom they considered to be following Islam properly and those who were not. As far as they concerned, the "moderates" were on the wrong side—and they continued to appeal to Muslims in the West on the basis of their claim that only the "extremists" were properly following the Qur'an and the example of Muhammad.

Meanwhile, those classified as "extremists," such as the famed jihad preacher in Britain, Anjem Choudary, skillfully exploited the weaknesses of the tolerant West:

> People like Anjem Choudhary were lawyers before they were practising Muslims, so they knew how the law works. Everyday they would study the latest version of the Anti-Terrorism Act [Law], and then call for Islamic law while staying within the guidelines of the British and Western law. This way, they could never be doing anything illegal while fulfilling the obligation of calling for Islam to be the highest.
>
> They would use the "freedom of expression" given to them to spread their beliefs. This put the European governments in a big dilemma.[582]

### The clash of civilizations is on

The European governments, the Islamic State claimed, solved this dilemma in an ingenious way:

So they plotted a new plot. If the Muslims were going to make "Shariah groups" which stay within the law, then they too will make "Anti-Shariah groups" which stay within the law. So rich anti-Islam people began funding far-right groups in different parts of the world whose only main focus is to fight Islam while staying within the guidelines of the law of the land.[583]

In a passage that was ironic in light of the Islamic State's sexual enslavement of hundreds of infidel women, *Black Flags from Rome* dismisses as "right-wing" propaganda the huge scandal in Britain of Muslim gangs sexually exploiting young non-Muslim girls:

> These charismatic leaders of right-wing groups would start to recruit more people to their causes, and protests, and would therefore receive even more funding. People who were normally neutral would start to receive their propaganda and start accepting it. The news media outlets would spread news that Muslim males were making "grooming gangs" which abuse "white girls", which would make even more people join the right-wing groups.[584]

The rising tensions set the stage for what was to come:

> In simple words, a clash of civilizations was occurring. A neo-Nazi order was forming in Europe as a reaction to real political Shari'ah-Islam. The future of Europe would be a violent one, until—"you will raid/attack Rome, and Allah will enable you to conquer it."[585]

The Syrian jihad enabled thousands of Muslims from Europe to become trained and battle-hardened: "Here they could learn basic armed/shooting combat, assassination techniques, how to make explosives from homemade materials etc."[586]

They would bring this training back to their home countries: "There were small armies of the Islamic State within every country of Europe by late 2014, and the intelligence agencies didn't even know about it! January 2015 was when these shocking secrets would be discovered, and all the world would see the depth of the Islamic State and Al Qa'idah infiltration in Europe."[587] Note the casual linking of the Islamic State and al-Qaeda, with no hint of antagonism between the two. The way the world discovered the "shocking secrets" was through the Kouachi brothers' massacre at the Charlie Hebdo offices in Paris.

## The left will help

These were not the only targets, of course. After describing the Charlie Hebdo and Hyper Cacher attacks in detail, the Islamic State explains how intelligence agencies collect huge amounts of data, "but they will not study it unless you are caught under the radar."[588] As attacks such as the ones in Paris become more common, law enforcement authorities will not be able to keep up:

> As the Western nations get poorer, their intelligence collection agencies will continue to exist, but they simply won't have enough manpower (less jobs) to analyse it all. With less attacks in the West being group (networked) attacks and an increasing amount of lone-wolf attacks, it will be more difficult for intelligence agencies to stop an increasing amount of violence and chaos from spreading in the West.[589]

As this violence and chaos spreads, leftist non-Muslim Europeans will help pave the way for the Islamic conquest of Europe, for "a growing population of left-winged activists (people who are against; human/animal abuses, Zionism, and Austerity measures etc.) look up to the Muslims as a force who are strong enough to fight against the injustices of the world. . . . Many of these people (who are sometimes part of Anonymous and Anarchy movements) will ally with the Muslims to fight against the neo-Nazis' and rich politicians. They will give intelligence, share weapons and do undercover work for the Muslims to pave the way for the conquest of Rome."

How would this happen? Leftist protesters would realize that taking up arms was their only viable alternative:

> If you have ever been at a pro-Palestine / anti-Israel protest, you will see many activists who are not even Muslims who are supportive of what Muslims are calling for (the fall of Zionism). It is most likely here that connections between Muslims and left-wing activists will be made, and a portion from them will realise that protests are not effective, and that armed combat is the alternative. So they will start to work together in small cells of groups to fight and sabotage against the "financial elite".[590]

*Black Flags from Rome* also explains "How to take, hold and expand territory," saying that "there are already 'Muslim No Go Zones' and even 'White only zones' existing within European countries," and explaining how

Muslims could steadily expand their zones of control, using the "main mosque" and the "Leader," until ultimately there is a "big national armed force of Muslim fighters. Muslim fighters from all European countries will continue the fight, breaking borders until they can reach; Northern Rome."[591]

The e-book details how to make Molotov cocktails and the kinds of bombs that the Tsarnaev brothers used in their jihad attack at the Boston Marathon. It also expresses confidence in the rather unlikely idea that Russia will aid the Muslims in conquering Europe. This exposes the entire plan as rather fanciful, but there is no doubt about one aspect of it: at least some Muslims in Europe will be committing murder in the name of Islam, jihad and the Islamic State in the near future.

There is nothing fanciful about that at all.

*Black Flags from Rome* ends with a series of photographs of the Coliseum and other Roman landmarks. It is at that point that the e-book starts to resemble a twisted tourist manual. But when the jihadis go sightseeing in Rome, they won't be armed with cameras and maps. The photographs are included so that once the jihadis do arrive, they will know where to go with their sledgehammers and drills.

Indeed, they are already there. Late in April 2015, Islamic State supporters in Rome and Milan tweeted photos of landmarks in each city, including the Coliseum in Rome, with a sign held in front of them reading, "We are on your streets, we are locating targets."[592]

## End times timetable

There is a timetable to all this. *Black Flags from Rome* begins with an epigraph consisting of a hadith in which Muhammad is depicted as saying that after the Muslims conquer Rome, the End Times would begin, with Muslims warring against the Anti-Christ:

> "You will raid/attack Arabia and Allah will give you victory over it, then you will raid/attack Persia (Iran) and Allah will give you victory over it, then you will raid Rome (Italy) and Allah will give you victory over it, then you will raid/attack al-Dajjal (the AntiChrist) and Allah will give you victory over him." [Saheeh Muslim [54/50].[593]

As far as the Islamic State is concerned, that is a prophecy that is certain to come true: first the jihadis will conquer Saudi Arabia, then Shi'ite Iran, and then Rome and Europe—at which point their battles will become eschatological, as they will fight and defeat the Dajjal, the Islamic version of the Antichrist, who will make war against the Muslim faithful before the second coming of Jesus Christ the Muslim Prophet and the consummation of all things.

In line with this, the Islamic State sees itself defeating Russia and Iran, whereupon the Romans—that is, the Europeans—would gather at Dabiq, a northern Syrian town. Why there? Because Muhammad is depicted in the hadith as also predicting that Dabiq would be the site of the final battle between the believers and the unbelievers:

> The Last Hour would not come until the Romans would land at al-A'maq or in Dabiq. An army consisting of the best (soldiers) of the people of the earth at that time will come from Medina (to counteract them). When they will arrange themselves in ranks, the Romans would say: Do not stand between us and those (Muslims) who took prisoners from amongst us. Let us fight with them; and the Muslims would say: Nay, by Allah, we would never get aside from you and from our brethren that you may fight them. They will then fight and a third (part) of the army would run away, whom Allah will never forgive. A third (part of the army) which would be constituted of excellent martyrs in Allah's eye, would be killed and the third who would never be put to trial would win and they would be conquerors of Constantinople.

Then, apparently the end would come, as Jesus the Muslim prophet (not to be confused with Jesus the Savior figure of Christianity) would then return to the earth and defeat the enemies of Allah:

> And as they would be busy in distributing the spoils of war (amongst themselves) after hanging their swords by the olive trees, the Satan would cry: The Dajjal [the Antichrist] has taken your place among your family. They would then come out, but it would be of no avail. And when they would come to Syria, he would come out while they would be still preparing themselves for battle drawing up the ranks. Certainly, the time of prayer shall come and then Jesus (peace be upon him) son of Mary would descend and would lead them in prayer. When the enemy of Allah would see him, it would (disappear) just as the salt dissolves itself in water and if he (Jesus) were not to confront them at all, even then it would dissolve

completely, but Allah would kill them by his hand and he would show them their blood on his lance (the lance of Jesus Christ).[594]

The Islamic State, taking all this as a certain foretelling of the future, says that the Europeans will "go on the offensive and arrive with 80 flags to Dabiq (near the Turkish/Syrian border), with more than 100,000 soldiers. This is when the great Malhama (Armageddon begins). It is such a big event that it is even mentioned in Christian Biblical scripture and refers to the time near Judgment Day."[595]

Whatever one believes in Christian or Muslim eschatology, that Judgment Day is coming, because the Islamic State is working toward it, and will continue to do so. The United States and the European Union, by contrast, prefer to continue to reassure themselves that this is not a religious war, or even a proper war at all, and that this whole thing will blow over fairly soon, once jihadis have jobs and social standing. But the Islamic State is confident that it will come down to a military showdown. *Black Flags from Rome* says that the European Union and the United States will fight the Islamic State at Dabiq, while "those who cannot reach Syria go on the offensive elsewhere depending on where they are located."

Around this time, the "puppet rulers in Muslim lands"—that is, rulers of Muslim countries who do not rule by Islamic law and pledge their allegiance to the new caliphate—"may be defeated." *Black Flags from Rome* predicts that this could happen by the year 2020—"equivalent to 100 years since the fall of the Ottoman Caliphate." If this happens, it will give "Islamic armed groups a lot of freedom to travel in Muslim lands, and on the Mediterranean sea, and also to use the airspace to target Europe with missiles they will have now captured from the Arab puppet regimes."[596]

The jihadis' timetable was derailed. But the initiative was not discarded. And Europe has so completely lost its identity and sense of itself—its pride, its rage at being invaded, the force of its reason in determining that the invasion should be resisted—that the conquest could prove easier than anyone on any side of the conflict has imagined. The German-language site Katholisches.info reported in April 2016 that "90 percent would convert to Islam without hesitation to save their own lives, [if] the Islamic State (IS) should conquer the country. This 'shock result' (Il Giornale) came from a survey of 13-year-olds at an Italian secondary school. Only two of 25 students opposed conversion. Both students are from devout Catholic families."[597]

This "shock result" came during a class discussion on the Islamic State (ISIS):

> The teacher gave them information. She told her students also that many fighters of the IS come from Europe. Young Muslims who are the second or third generation immigrants. They are well integrated, come from families with a certain level of prosperity, and several possess a university degree or have begun studies. One of the most infamous executioners of IS was previously a well-known DJ in Europe.

The teacher reportedly did not sugarcoat the Islamic State's hostility to Christians and Christianity: "The teacher told her students that the IS destroyed all Christian symbols and threatened everyone who was not willing to convert to Islam with death. She also did not conceal that many Christians were killed, exiled or enslaved because of their faith by IS."

If the teacher intended this news to make the students resolute in the defense of their ancestral religion and culture, however, it had the opposite effect: all but the two devout Catholic students agreed that if the Islamic State confronted them, they would surrender rather than fight, and would convert to Islam.

This was just one classroom in one school. But there is no reason to assume that the answer would be significantly different in most schools all over continental Europe, as well as in Britain and even in the United States. Schools where students are taught to value their own cultural heritage, and to be ready to fight to defend it, are rare indeed—in publicly funded schools all over the West, curricula that taught such a thing would be denounced as "racist" and "xenophobic" and wouldn't last long if they were implemented at all.

These children in this Italian classroom are the products of a relativistic, materialistic, hedonistic culture that has relentlessly indoctrinated them with the ideas that all belief systems and cultures are of equal value and are essentially interchangeable, and that it is wrong and "racist" to oppose even an authoritarian and violent ideology, and that defense of one's homeland and culture is likewise "racist," and that Judeo-Christian Western civilization is itself uniquely "racist" and responsible for the great majority of the evil in the world.

## The black flag of Islam: Omar Bakri and Abu Hamza

The Islamic State was by no means the first Islamic group to state that it wanted to conquer and Islamize Europe. Some Muslim leaders were forthright about their intentions years ago. In the early years of the 21st century in England, Abu Hamza al-Masri, the forbidding one-eyed, hook-handed imam of the notorious Finsbury Park mosque (which shoe bomber Richard Reid, al-Qaeda conspirator Zacharias Moussaoui, and other suspected terrorists are said to have frequented), praised the September 11 terrorist attacks:

> If it was done because people are desperate and their lives have been threatened, then that is a respectable cause which no one could dare to condemn. Then those people who carried out the attacks would be martyrs. Martyrdom is the highest form of jihad (holy war). If you do things for the cause of God, losing your life for it is the highest form of pure belief. This is in the Koran. America thinks that it comes first, but Muslims believe that a believer comes first.[598] [The explanatory parenthetical defining jihad is in the original CNN story.]

Abu Hamza has also declared that "Bin Laden is a good guy. Everyone likes him in the Muslim world, there is nothing wrong with the man and his beliefs."[599] And he praised al-Qaeda terrorist attacks on American embassies in Kenya and Tanzania: "If Muslims are having a war against these people, than yes, it is legitimate."[600]

Early in 2003, Scotland Yard raided Abu Hamza's mosque on suspicion that terrorists were operating there. According to police spokesmen, the raid was linked to arrests made several weeks earlier of Muslims who were producing the poison ricin—evidently also "for the cause of God."[601]

Before he was stripped of his British citizenship (he is now in prison in the United States for trying to establish an al-Qaeda training camp in Bly, Oregon), Hamza headed up an organization called Supporters of Sharia, which like al-Muhajiroun was dedicated to establishing Islamic rule on the Sceptered Isle. Like other Muslim radicals, he, too, stated that even though he was a British citizen, he was not in fact British, but Muslim. In addresses to his followers, Hamza has said, "If a kafir person (non-believer) goes in a Muslim country, he is like a cow. Anybody can take him. That is the Islamic law. . . . If a kafir is walking by and you catch him, he's booty. You can sell him in the market. Most of them are spies. And even if they don't do anything, if

Muslims cannot take them and sell them in the market, you just kill them. It's OK."[602]

When challenged about these and other outrageous remarks, Hamza claimed he was quoted out of context and then said, "I say the reality that's in the Muslim books anyway. Whether I say it or not, it's in the books."[603]

Another jihadi cleric, Sheikh Omar Bakri Muhammad, boasted about exploiting the contradiction between freedom of speech and self-preservation. He openly declared his intention to "transform the West into Dar Al-Islam" and establish Sharia on British soil.[604] "I want to see the black flag of Islam flying over Downing Street," he said, and his al-Muhajiroun group was dedicated to this goal.[605] That was, in fact, the name of Bakri's daughter: the Black Flag of Islam.[606]

Bakri explained that the transformation of Britain into an Islamic state could come about by means of an "invasion [from] without"; in that case, he said, "if an Islamic state arises and invades [the West] we will be its army and its soldiers from within."[607] But if no such Islamic state arises, Bakri says that Muslims will convert the West to Islam "through ideological invasion . . . without war and killing."[608]

When asked how he could say such things while enjoying the protections of British citizenship, Bakri was sanguine. "As long as my words do not become actions, they do no harm. Here, the law does not punish you for words, as long as there is no proof you have carried out actions. In such a case you are still on the margins of the law, and they cannot punish you. If they want to punish you, they must present evidence against you, otherwise their laws will be in a state of internal contradiction."[609]

Bakri said that if he was punished for things he was saying, he planned to exploit this contradiction. "We will be able to claim that the capitalist camp has failed in the face of the Islamic camp in actualizing the things in which it believes, like freedom of expression. . . . We must prove that man-made law is a fragile law. . . . Allah said, 'Do not obey the infidels and the hypocrites.'"[610]

Ultimately, Omar Bakri left Britain for a visit to his native Lebanon and was not allowed to return. But his absence from Britain, and the outlawing of his al-Muhajiroun group, did not mean that the imperative for Islamic conquest had vanished from the country.

What's more, the effects of Bakri's teachings were felt in other parts of the world as well. Asif Mohammed Hanif, a British citizen who was Bakri's student in England, demonstrated the fragility of manmade law on April 30, 2003, in Tel Aviv. After posing as a peace activist in Israel, he killed three people in a suicide bombing attack at a bar near the American embassy.[611] Hanif's accomplice, Omar Khan Sharif, who was also one of Bakri's former students, failed to detonate his bomb and escaped, although his body later washed up on a Tel Aviv beach under mysterious circumstances.[612]

Bakri himself refused to condemn the attack: "There is no way for me to condemn the self-sacrificing operation that took place in Palestine against occupying forces."[613] However, Iqbal Sacranie of the Muslim Council of Britain**Error! Bookmark not defined.** disagreed: "Let us be absolutely clear, the loss of innocent life is against the laws of humanity."[614]

Some of Sharif's neighbors in Derby wondered at what the *New York Times* described as "the radicalization of the well-educated, thoroughly Westernized Mr. Sharif, 27."[615] Hamida Akhtar, a longtime acquaintance of Sharif noted a change in the would-be suicide bomber. "'He used to be dressed like this,' Ms. Akhtar said, pointing to her husband, Mohammed, who was wearing a suit and tie. 'Suddenly, he was changed.' He had a new wife, too, named Tahira Tabassum, who wore a traditional Islamic head scarf."[616]

Other Derby Muslims, however, seemed to understand Sharif's actions perfectly well. A young man named Basu Hussain said, "What he's done is very good, and they won't ever find him. We should all get together and kill all the Jews."[617] Shaban Yasin, 17, agreed, but wasn't sure that suicide bombing was the best means to that end. "We should find out the best way to kill them, and do that." Yasan opined that if he himself became a suicide bomber, "I think my parents would be proud of me."[618]

Another Muslim in Britain, Shakil Muhammad, said that he would be willing to follow in the footsteps of Hanif and Sharif by becoming a suicide bomber as well: "I would volunteer: more and more people will follow him. To be a martyr in our religion is a great honour. It's only a matter of time before somebody blows themselves up in this country—that will definitely happen. I'm somebody who really believes in this, but the picture is bigger than me. We are going to make a change."[619]

Others admired Hanif and Sharif without committing himself to imitate them: "Killing people is wrong, obviously, but if he was doing it for God himself—then fair enough. . . . You have to be pretty brave to do something like that, to hold a bomb in your hand and blow yourself up."[620]

## The murder of Lee Rigby

The most notorious effect of Omar Bakri's preaching in Britain was the murder of a British soldier on a London street in May 2013 by a former member of al-Muhajiroun. Michael Adebolajo, a convert to Islam who called himself Mujaheed, his hands scarlet with the blood of Drummer Lee Rigby, the British soldier he had just brutally murdered on a London street, and still holding the tools of his murder, approached a television cameraman and calmly began explaining himself.

In the course of his explanation, Adebolajo invoked the Qur'an's ninth chapter (*Surat at-Tawba*), which enjoins Muslims to make war against and subjugate Jews and Christians, declaring, "we are forced by the Qur'an, in Sura At-Tawba, through many ayah [verses] in the Qur'an, we must fight them as they fight us." He added: "I apologize that women had to witness this today but in our lands women have to see the same."

Adebolajo's reference to "our lands" may have appeared odd, as Adebolajo's parents were Nigerians who had immigrated to England in the early 1980s. But he meant neither English nor Nigerian lands, of course; Adebolajo converted to Islam around 2003, and that meant that in his mind he was no longer English, if he ever had been. He understood his commitment to Islam to supersede everything else, demanding a loyalty above national allegiances and even ties of kith and kin. The Qur'an commands Muslims to "be good to parents" (17:22). However, even in that relationship, the overarching principle is that Muslims must be "hard against the unbelievers, merciful one to another" (48:29).

And so Mujaheed Michael Adebolajo committed murder on a street of the land where he grew up in defense of those he considered to be his only true kith and kin: Muslims worldwide. He did so, moreover, in obedience to what he considered to be the commands of his holy book.

British government and media elites, however, were sure that he had gotten his religion all wrong. Unsurprisingly, they rushed to assure the public that Islam had nothing to do with his action. Adebolajo was an "extremist" who misunderstood the clear and peaceful teachings of Islam. British Prime Minister David Cameron summed up the mainstream view when he said in the House of Commons,

> What happened on the streets of Woolwich shocked and sickened us all. It was a despicable attack on a British soldier who stood for our country and our way of life and it was too a betrayal of Islam and of

the Muslim communities who give so much to our country. There is nothing in Islam that justifies acts of terror and I welcome the spontaneous condemnation of this attack from Mosques and community organisations right across our country.[621]

Muslim organizations did indeed condemn the murder, but that in itself did not necessarily establish that it was a betrayal of Islam; Muslim organizations may have condemned the murder because they thought it was inopportune, or because they thought it was politically necessary to do so. Whatever their genuine sentiments about it, however, their condemnations reinforced Cameron's core belief that Islam was a peaceful religion that was not represented by its "extremists." This complacency boded ill for Europe's ability to deal realistically with the threat it had brought upon itself.

Demographic trends suggest that Islamic rule could be established in the Netherlands and other countries of Western Europe without violent conquest. The Muslim population of Europe doubled between 1989 and 1998, and if population trends continue, Holland could have a Muslim majority by 2040 or earlier. A Muslim France could emerge by the same year. According to journalist Christopher Caldwell, the French government

> now estimates its Muslim population at 4 to 5 million. Most social scientists believe this number is too low, speaking of as many as 8 million Muslims in France (and 12 to 20 million in the European Union). These numbers underestimate the weight of French Islam, since the population is concentrated and—thanks to a birthrate that, while falling, remains a multiple of the native-French one— extremely young. In parts of Paris, Marseilles, Rhone-Alpes, and Strasbourg, between a third and half of people in their teens and twenties are Muslim.[622]

There are significant and growing Muslim populations in other Western European countries as well.

Yet despite all the societal upheaval that the migrant influx had caused, the British government declared in June 2019 that it planned to "resettle thousands more refugees starting from next year, and for years to come."[623] Home Secretary Sajid Javid bragged that "since 2016, Britain has resettled more refugees than any other EU state, something that we're very proud of."[624]

Similarly, in January 2018, United Nations refugee chief Filippo Grandi stated, "We need to work more with Europe, and other countries that receive refugees, to make reception systems more effective for larger numbers than before."[625] The influx was just beginning.

## *The fork in the road*

As mass migration continued but populists increased in popularity, Europe was at a crossroads. And its growing Muslim communities faced what may have been the starkest choice of all: would they ultimately accept the secular framework developed by the Christians and post-Christians of Europe, or would they adopt a more confrontational course and hold fast to their Muslim traditions?

The utter opposition of these two worlds showed vividly in their differing ideas even of what constitutes acceptable dialogue. Driven by ideas of tolerance that are based in Judeo-Christian and Enlightenment ideas of human dignity, Europeans are trying to stave off a confrontation between Muslims and non-Muslims in Europe. Some Muslim leaders, however, are eager for that confrontation.

These lines were drawn and differences delineated as far back as May 1999, when Pope John Paul II, in a spectacular and controversial act, kissed the Qur'an during an audience with Muslim leaders and the Chaldean Catholic Patriarch of Babylon (Baghdad). For this, the Pope was criticized by his Catholic flock and other Christians; yet however ill-advised his kiss might have been, it showed how serious he was about having peaceful relations with Muslims. During a visit to the Umayyad mosque in Damascus, he said, "It is my ardent hope that Muslim and Christian religious leaders and teachers will present our two great religious communities as communities in respectful dialogue, never more as communities in conflict. It is crucial for the young to be taught the ways of respect and understanding, so that they will not be led to misuse religion itself to promote or justify hatred and violence."[626]

Yet while the Pope's words reflected the general sentiments of most in the West, this generosity was never wholeheartedly reciprocated among Muslims. Some Muslim leaders took umbrage at the very idea of rapprochement between Christians and Muslims; it offended their conviction that Islam embodies the last and greatest revelation from Allah. Accordingly, in a sermon in Mecca, the Saudi Sheikh Adnan Ahmad Siyami denounced the Pope's initiative:

Several years ago, a sinful call arose, which unfortunately garnered support from some clerics and preachers of this religion, Islam . . . [a call] for the unification of the monotheistic religions. . . . This call will lead . . . to presenting the infidels' schools of thought as correct, and to silence regarding them; to permitting conversion to Judaism and Christianity with no shame whatsoever; to the abolition of the vast difference between the Muslims and others—a difference underpinning the conflict between truth and falsehood.

Siyami found this "sinful call" embodied in the Pope's statements in Syria:

The Pope's recent visit to Syria, to the Al-Umawi mosque is, without a doubt, another manifestation of that call. The call by [the Pope]— may Allah punish him as he deserves—to the people of the [different] religions in Syria to live in peaceful coexistence is nothing more than an audacious call for the unification of religions, in accordance with the principle of human religious harmony. . . . Can we expect compassion from these murderous wolves? What made the Pope go on his visit was his dissatisfaction with the robbing of the Muslims' lands; he wanted also to rob their religion, so that they lose both this world and the Hereafter.[627]

With some Muslim leaders holding such views, what would become of Christian and post-Christian Europe when its Muslim minorities became majorities? Yet despite the manifest transformation of Europe that the migrant influx had wrought, if one didn't accept the brave new world that was sure to bring more jihad and more Sharia to the continent, the charges of being a Nazi and a racist came quickly.

So what did anyone expect? Did anyone in Europe or anywhere else really think that the migrants who had repeatedly shown their contempt for European society, law, and culture would come to love their new countries and be willing to fight to defend them? Would the native Europeans who had been taught to despise their own cultures and histories fight to save their nations from hostile invaders? It was much more likely that they would be glad to be subjugated, so as to assuage their guilt over being the children and heirs of the world's colonialists and enslavers. They have never been taught, and will not be taught, that their new Muslim overlords are in fact the exponents of a culture that has been far more imperialist and more deeply involved in slavery than the West ever was.

As they get used to the dehumanization of women and institutionalized discrimination against non-Muslims, these young denizens of Islamizing Europe will console themselves with the lessons they learned in school about how Islam inspired a great and tolerant civilization in Al-Andalus and led numerous people to glorious innovations in science, philosophy, and more. It will likely never occur to them, since they have never been taught how to think critically, that the Islamic civilization that is asserting control over their homeland and all of Europe is nothing like what they were taught in school to expect, as it is not really either great or tolerant, and is quite hostile to intellectual endeavors that are deemed un-Islamic—which happens all too often.

Even if that subversive thought does cross some of their minds, by then it will be far too late, as most of their classmates will indeed have converted and joined the religion of the overlords, and the rest are rapidly learning to make the necessary adjustments to get along. The Christian remnant in Egypt, and Syria, and Pakistan learned how to do that, adjusting to a precarious existence in which one's life could be forfeit if one did not show the requisite "respect" to Muslims whenever and wherever and however that respect was demanded. The Christians and post-Christians of Europe will learn how to do so as well. And many will discover, to their surprise and relief, that it is actually quite easy to live as a slave. Once one accepts the fact that freedom is gone, one can savor that responsibility is as well. What could be sweeter?

Meanwhile, no one has even bothered to ask, much less answer, one central question: why is it incumbent upon Europe have to absorb all these refugees? Why not Saudi Arabia or the other Muslim countries that are oil-rich and have plenty of space? The answer is unspoken because non-Muslim authorities refuse to believe it and Muslims don't want it stated or known: these refugees have to go to Europe because this is a Hijrah. In doing so, they are abetted by European internationalists who either don't know or don't care about the implications of what they are doing.

This could be Europe's death knell.

## *The policy of appeasement returns*

In late March 2020, when the government of France announced new penalties for those who ignored quarantine regulations during the coronavirus pandemic, the Secretary of State to the Minister of the Interior,

Laurent Nuñez, made a telling exception. "It is not a priority to enforce closings in certain neighborhoods and to stop gatherings," wrote Nuñez, referring to the no-go areas with heavy concentrations of Muslim migrants.[628]

French police were dismayed. Rocco Contento, a police union leader in France, declared that Nuñez's order was "incredible," adding that the no-go areas were the precise areas where police "find it most difficult to enforce the quarantine. . . . Colleagues are literally assaulted during checks. A police officer was even bitten in Clichy-sous-Bois."[629] It was, however, impossible to have a rational public discussion about such matters. After noting that police found it hardest to enforce the quarantine in heavily migrant areas, Contento added, "But if we say that, we are immediately racist. However, this is a fact." Nuñez, however, argued that if the quarantine were enforced too strictly in these areas, riots could break out.

The concept of appeasement is usually applied to conflicts between nation-states, with the most infamous example being the attempt by Great Britain and France to appease Nazi Germany just before World War II. Despite its dismal 20th-century record, however, appeasement has again become the diplomatic weapon of choice for many European government officials—this time not in the context of war between nations, but as a way to deal with restive, growing, and unassimilated Muslim populations within their own countries.

It may be astounding to informed onlookers that Europe would again be pursuing a policy of appeasement in any context. But hindsight is easy; in the 19th century, appeasement was an effective policy to which all the Great Powers had recourse at one time or another. The difference between the 19th century and the 1930s was that in the earlier period, the West was appeasing from a position of strength, not weakness. In the 1930s, Britain and France were both war-weary and horrified by the pointless carnage of World War I. In that environment, it seemed reasonable to make concessions, even ones with significant political ramifications, in order to ensure a lasting peace. Increasing sentiment in both countries that the Treaty of Versailles had been unjust to the Germans, and that those injustices needed to be redressed, compounded these sentiments.

Appeasement-minded politicians, therefore, believed that the course they were pursuing would heal the long-standing enmity between Germany and the Western democracies and head off another world war. On September 27, 1938, British Prime Minister Neville Chamberlain explained and defended the appeasement policy in an address to the British people and a speech in the House of Commons. He positioned himself as the representative of those who were deeply worried by the prospect of another world war:

> First of all I must say something to those who have written to my wife or myself in these last weeks to tell us of their gratitude for my efforts and to assure us of their prayers for my success. Most of these letters have come from women—mothers or sisters of our own countrymen. But there are countless others besides—from France, from Belgium, from Italy, even from Germany, and it has been heartbreaking to read of the growing anxiety they reveal and their intense relief when they thought, too soon, that the danger of war was past.

He went on, infamously: "If I felt my responsibility heavy before, to read such letters has made it seem almost overwhelming. How horrible, fantastic, incredible it is that we should be digging trenches and trying on gas masks here because of a quarrel in a far-away country between people of whom we know nothing." If a world war must break out, he suggested that it should be over something more important than the territorial integrity of Czechoslovakia: "If we have to fight it must be on larger issues than that." He told the Commons that he was being inundated with letters from people who were asking "if they were asked to go to war in order that the Sudeten Germans might not join the Reich." He claimed that by dismembering Czechoslovakia, he was saving it from "annihilation" and giving it "a chance of new life as a new State, which involves the loss of territory and fortifications, but may perhaps enable her to enjoy in the future and develop a national existence under a neutrality and security comparable to that which we see in Switzerland to-day."[630]

The parallels with the present situation are many, even though in the global jihad today, Europe doesn't face a conventional threat from a nation-state. Nevertheless, Sharia supremacists wish to transform Western European societies and remake them in their own image no less thoroughly than did the Nazis. And after World War II, Vietnam, and the Cold War, the West in general is just as war-weary, if not more so, than Europe was in the 1930s. Recalling the dissatisfaction in the democracies with the Versailles Treaty and the devastation it had wrought upon the German economy, many influential politicians in both Europe and the United States believe that the foreign policy posture of the United States and Britain since September 11,

2001, has been unjust to the Islamic world—and unjust to the extent that it has created resentments that would disappear if this posture were abandoned.

Add to this mix a multiculturalist ethos that exalts the presence of foreign and non-assimilated cultures within Western countries perceived as large umbrella structures for a huge variety of diverse peoples, and the stage is set for a policy of appeasement of political agenda and the ideology of Islamic supremacism. European elites today believe that by admitting large numbers of Muslim immigrants into their country and making special accommodations for Islamic culture and practices, Europe will achieve a new cultural flowering—but left unconsidered in this is the nature of political Islam, which when dominant is hardly hospitable to rival political systems or cultures.

Cultural appeasement has become the norm in Europe today. The old model of requiring that immigrants assimilate and adopt the customs and mores of their new country has given way to a multiculturalist model that envisions immigrants maintaining their own practices and cultural habits in their new country. In the case of Islam, since Islamic law contains a complete model for society and governance that is considered to be divinely inspired and superior to all its rivals, multiculturalism accommodation is short-sighted and tantamount to cultural suicide. And given that Islam also is unique among the religions of the world in containing a developed doctrine, theology, and legal system that mandate warfare against unbelievers, this accommodation is difficult to distinguish, either in intention or effect, from outright appeasement.

If Western Europe does become Islamized, as demographic trends suggest, before too long America will be facing a world that is drastically different and more forbidding than today's. And the same process of Islamization will proceed here—unless enough people wake up in time to head it off. The Muslim population in the United States is much smaller than that of Western Europe. The active  supremacists among them are even smaller in number.

Nonetheless, the same things that have happened in Europe could easily happen in the United States.

# CHAPTER 9

## WHAT THE U.S. CAN AND SHOULD LEARN FROM MASS MIGRATION IN EUROPE

The unfolding of all this contains numerous lessons for the United States in dealing with its own immigration questions. Bat Ye'or correctly noted that

> Americans must discuss the tragic development of Eurabia, and its profound implications for the United States, particularly in terms of its resultant foreign policy realities. Americans should consider the despair and confusion of many Europeans, prisoners of a Eurabian totalitarianism that foments a culture of deadly lies about Western civilization. Americans should know that this self-destructive calamity did not just happen, rather it was the result of deliberate policies, executed and monitored by ostensibly responsible people. Finally, Americans should understand that Eurabia's contemporary anti-Zionism and anti-Americanism are the spiritual heirs of 1930s Nazism and anti-Semitism, triumphally resurgent.[631]

Bat Ye'or concluded, "The cracks between Europe and America reveal the divergences between the choice of liberty and the road back to Munich on which the European Union continues to caper to new Arab-Islamic tunes, now called 'occupation,' 'peace and justice,' and 'immigrants' rights'—themes which were composed for Israel's burial. And for Europe's demise."[632]

That divergence between the choice of liberty and the road back to Munich was also apparent in the policies of Presidents Barack Obama and Donald Trump. Despite what he termed the "setback" of the November 2015 Islamic State jihad massacre in Paris, Barack Obama announced days after the attack that he was pressing forward with his scheme to flood the U.S. with at least 10,000 refugees from Syria, terming opposition to his plan "shameful."[633]

"We have to, each of us, do our part, and the United States has to step up and do its part," Obama said.[634] He didn't explain why Saudi Arabia, the United Arab Emirates, and Qatar didn't have to do their part and had taken no refugees at all, citing the risk of terrorism.[635] Obama had harsh words for those who opposed his plan: "When I hear folks say that, well, maybe we should just admit the Christians but not the Muslims. When I hear political leaders suggesting that there would be a religious test for which person who's fleeing from a war-torn country is admitted. When some of those folks themselves come from families who benefitted from protection when they were fleeing political persecution—That's shameful. That's not American. That's not who we are. We don't have religious tests to our compassion."[636]

Indeed. But there were other issues that did not involve "religious tests to our compassion." Obama's statement ignored the uncomfortable fact that Christians were not waging jihad around the world. Robert Bentley, the Governor of Alabama, was more realistic, explaining that he did not want any of the refugees in Alabama because "I will not stand complicit to a policy that places the citizens of Alabama in harm's way."[637] The Governor of Texas, Greg Abbott, noted that "a Syrian 'refugee' appears to have been part of the Paris terror attack. American humanitarian compassion could be exploited to expose Americans to similar deadly danger."[638] Arkansas Governor Asa Hutchinson stated that taking Syrian refugees at this time "is not the right strategy."[639] Even the Governor of Massachusetts, Charlie Baker, came out against Obama's plan: "No, I'm not interested in accepting refugees from Syria," he said.[640] "My view on this is the safety and security of the people of the Commonwealth of Mass. is my highest priority. So I would set the bar very high on this."[641]

Obama brushed all such concerns aside: "The people who are fleeing Syria," he asserted, "are the most harmed by terrorism.... It is very important . . . that we do not close our hearts to these victims of such violence and somehow start equating the issue of refugees with the issue of terrorism."[642] He didn't address the possibility that jihadis might be among the refugees, but Deputy National Security Adviser Ben Rhodes attempted to reassure the American people by claiming that the Obama Administration had "very extensive screening procedures" to weed out jihadis from among the refugees.[643] Former NATO Supreme Commander James Stavridis also claimed that U.S. officials would be able to vet the refugees "safely and appropriately."[644] He added, "We should continue to take a substantial number of Syrian refugees because it is the right thing to do for the international community and because over time they will prove to be citizens of real capability and true grit, like many who immigrated before them in troubled times. The key is serious vetting using all the tools at our disposal."645

Yet FBI director James Comey was not so sanguine about the possibility of vetting the refugees: "If we have no information on someone, they've never crossed our radar screen . . . it will be challenging," he said—and most jihadis from Syria had not crossed the U.S. radar screen, as the U.S. had not had a military presence there comparable to that in Iraq.646

Also, the problem was much larger than the possibility of terrorists among the refugees. It was one of the preservation of the culture and civilization of the host countries. President Donald Trump, who acted in numerous ways to slow the migrant influx into the United States, seemed to understand that in a way his predecessor never showed any indication of doing.

Speaking in Poland in July 2017, President Trump delivered a ringing affirmation that he would defend Western civilization: "Just as Poland could not be broken, I declare today for the world to hear that the West will never, ever be broken. Our values will prevail, our people will thrive, and our civilization will triumph."647

Trump's remarkable innovation and sharp departure from the example his predecessor set was in declaring that *Western* civilization would triumph. Barack Hussein Obama, by contrast, was famous for declaring the triumph of *Islamic* civilization, most notably when he told the United Nations General Assembly on September 25, 2012, "The future must not belong to those who slander the prophet of Islam."648

If the future was not to belong to those who were perceived as slandering the prophet of Islam, Sharia blasphemy laws criminalizing criticism of Islam would have to have been imposed; people weren't likely to give up criticizing Muhammad voluntarily, especially as jihad terror attacks incited by his teachings become an ever more common feature of life in the West. Thus, if the future didn't belong to those who slander the prophet of Islam, it would be because freedom of speech had been extinguished and Islamic values had prevailed: Islamic civilization would have triumphed. Europe is already on the way to this.

Trump offered a radically different vision. "We are fighting hard against radical Islamic terrorism," he declared.649 "And we will prevail. We cannot accept those who reject our values and who use hatred to justify violence against the innocent."650

Robert Spencer

Trump in Warsaw wasn't just paying lip service to unattainable ideals, any more than Obama was when he said that "the future must not belong to those who slander the prophet of Islam." Obama worked very hard to make sure that would be true, and now Trump is working just as hard to ensure that Judeo-Christian civilization survives instead. Americans can be grateful that we do not, for the moment, have (as Trump has said) a president of the world, but a president of the United States. In light of what has happened in Europe, this could be the difference between civilizational survival and extinction.

---

ROBERT SPENCER is the director of Jihad Watch and a Shillman Fellow at the David Horowitz Freedom Center. He is the author of 19 books, including the *New York* Times bestsellers *The Politically Incorrect Guide to Islam (and the Crusades)* and *The Truth About Muhammad.* His latest book is *The Palestinian Delusion: The Catastrophic History of the Middle East Peace Process.*

# REFERENCES

1 "Europa wird am Ende des Jahrhunderts islamisch sein," *Die Welt*, July 28, 2004.

2 Steve Harrigan, "Swedes Reach Muslim Breaking Point," Fox News, November 26, 2004.

3 "100 percent immigrants at Danish school," DR Nyheder, September 9, 2004.

4 "Islam part of core curriculum in Danish schools," DR Nyheder, September 13, 2004.

5 "Bin Laden backer on his way to Oslo," Aftenposten, August 9, 2004.

6 "Qazi Hussain Ahmed refused to comment on capital punishment on blasphemy and homosexuality during visit to Norway," *Pakistan Christian Post*, September 9, 2004.

7 "Secret arrests as Dutch terror threat 'worse than thought,'" *Expatica*, September 14, 2004.

8 "Row as Muslim prisoners take on governors," *Expatica*, September 9, 2004; Giles Tremlett, "Spanish jail wing 'run by inmates,'" *The Guardian*, September 10, 2004.

9 Melissa Eddy, "Angela Merkel Calls for European Unity to Address Migrant Influx," New York Times, August 31, 2015.

10 Justin Huggler, "Merkel defiant over refugee policy: 'we can do it,'" Telegraph, August 31, 2016.

11 "Turkish FM warns of 'religion wars' in Europe in remarks on Dutch elections," Hürriyet Daily News, March 16, 2017.

12 Robert Spencer, "The Rise of Eurabia," FrontPage Magazine, March 30, 2004.

13 Ibid.

14 Bat Ye'or, "Eurabia: The Road to Munich," in Robert Spencer, editor, *The Myth of Islamic Tolerance: How Islamic Law Treats Non-Muslims*, Prometheus, 2004, p. 290.

15 Ibid., pp. 290–291.

16 Ibid., p. 291.

17 Ibid., p. 290.

18 Robert Spencer, "The Rise of Eurabia."

19 Ibid.

20 Bat Ye'or, "How Europe Became Eurabia," FrontPage, July 27, 2004.

21 Ibid.

22 Ibid.

23 Bat Ye'or: "Beyond Munich: The Spirit of Eurabia," in Robert Spencer, editor, *The Myth of Islamic Tolerance: How Islamic Law Treats Non-Muslims*, Prometheus, 2004, pp. 284–285.

24 "Mideast conflict must not hinder Med Union-Sarkozy," Reuters, April 30, 2008.

25 Ibid.

26 Bat Ye'or, "Eurabia: The Road to Munich," p. 291.

27 Ibid., p. 292.

28 Bat Ye'or, "How Europe Became Eurabia."

29 Ibid.

30 Ibid.

31 Ibid.

32 Ibid.

33 Ibid.

34 "Fox News apologizes for European Muslim population errors," Fox News, January 18, 2015.

35 Jay Bookman, "Fox News admits 'no-go zones' are fantasy," Atlanta Journal-Constitution, January 19, 2015.

36 "Fox Pundits Finally 'Apologize' After A Week Of Being Mocked For 'No Go Zones' Claim," Crooks and Liars, January 18, 2015.

37 Robert Mackey, "Fox News Apologizes for False Claims of Muslim-Only Areas in England and France," New York Times, January 18, 2015.

38 "More Than A Week Later, Fox Admits It Was Kinda Sorta Wrong About 'No Go Zones,'" NewsHounds, January 17, 2015.

39 Stephen Castle and Robert Mackey, "Fox News Beats a Retreat After Gaffes About Islam," New York Times, January 12, 2015.

40 Dan Bloom and Tom McTague, "Cameron brands Fox News terror expert a 'complete idiot' after claiming Birmingham is 'totally Muslim' and 'non-Muslims just simply don't go in,'" MailOnline, January 11, 2015.

41 Ibid.

42 Ibid.

43 Michael Nazir-Ali, "Extremism flourished as UK lost Christianity," Telegraph, January 11, 2008.

44 Caroline Gammell, "Muslims call for 'no-go' CoE bishop to resign," Telegraph, April 18, 2008.

45 "British bishop says he faces threats after comments on Islamic extremism," Associated Press, February 3, 2008.

46 Michael Evans, "Military uniforms in public 'risk offending minorities,'" Times of London, March 8, 2008.

47 Jamie Doward, "Revealed: preachers' messages of hate: Muslim worshippers are being urged by radical clerics to ignore British law," The Observer, January 7, 2007.

48 "Fox News apologizes for European Muslim population errors," Fox News, January 18, 2015.

49 Stephen Castle and Robert Mackey, "Fox News Beats a Retreat After Gaffes About Islam,".

50 Rebecca Camber, "'No porn or prostitution': Islamic extremists set up Sharia law controlled zones in British cities," Daily Mail, July 28, 2011.

51 K. Elsner, "'Muslim Patrol' Sent to Jail for Enforcing Sharia Law in London Streets," Guardian Liberty Voice, December 7, 2013.

52 "VIDEO: Fresh footage of 'Muslim patrols' emerges online," The Docklands & East London Advertiser, February 5, 2013.

[53] "US student scarred in east London bottle attack," BBC, October 23, 2013.

[54] Mark Duell, "'This is a Muslim area and we don't want to see that': Mob pelts brothers-in-law wearing mankinis on sponsored walk with stones and accuses them of being paedophiles," Daily Mail, August 6, 2013.

[55] Liam Deacon, "UK: Whites Scared, White-Owned Businesses Stoned in a Racially Divided Bradford 'Heading for Disaster'" Breitbart, December 24, 2017.

[56] Ibid.

[57] Ibid.

[58] Ibid.

[59] David Ignatius, "Wake up to the problem: Separate and unequal in France," International Herald Tribune, April 27, 2002.

[60] Christopher Dickey, "Europe's Time Bomb," Newsweek, November 20, 2005.

[61] Donald Morrison, "What Does It Mean to Be French? The 'Charlie Hebdo' Massacre Complicates the Answer," New Republic, January 8, 2015.

[62] Daniel Pipes, "The 751 No-Go Zones of France," DanielPipes.org, November 14, 2006.

[63] Paul Belien, "'Sensitive urban areas,'" *Washington Times*, January 16, 2008.

[64] Virginia Hale, "Korea Warns Against Visiting Paris Migrant Suburbs After Men Loot, Try to Set Fire to Coach of Tourists," Breitbart, February 14, 2017.

[65] Chris Tomlinson, "No Go Zones: Chaperone-Matching App Helps Protect Travellers from Assaults in Paris," Breitbart, March 2, 2018.

[66] Chris Tomlinson, "Morocco Police to Patrol Paris Streets to Tackle Migrant Youth Gangs," Breitbart, July 20, 2018.

[67] Chris Tomlinson, "Residents of Swedish 'No Go Zone' Suburbs Afraid to Leave Their Homes," Breitbart, November 21, 2017.

[68] Chris Tomlinson, "80 Per Cent Of Swedish Police Consider Quitting Over Migrant Danger," Breitbart, September 20, 2016.

[69] Ibid.

[70] Ibid.

[71] Chris Tomlinson, "Sweden: New 'No Go Zone' Police Station Rammed by Car, Attacked by Masked Arsonists," Breitbart, August 8, 2018.

[72] Chris Tomlinson, "Sweden: No-Go Areas Hire Security Guards to Make up for Lack of Police," Breitbart, September 8, 2019.

[73] Chris Tomlinson, "Residents of Swedish 'No Go Zone' Suburbs Afraid to Leave Their Homes," Breitbart, November 21, 2017.

[74] Chris Tomlinson, "Researcher Blames Multiculturalism for Rise of Arab Clan Gangs in Germany," Breitbart, March 10, 2019.

[75] Vincent Wood, "Police say they are 'sick' of citizens' NO-GO ZONE fears as terrified Germans beg for help," Express, October 13, 2016.

[76] Ibid.

[77] Ibid.

[78] Ibid.

[79] "'You have to call it by name': Merkel publicly admits 'no-go areas' in Germany," RT, February 27, 2018.

80 "Belgian laws do not interest him. The man is confident that it is he who controls the neighborhood," Jihad Watch, September 5, 2007.

81 Julian Robinson, "Angela Merkel under more pressure over refugee policy as it is revealed migrants committed 142,500 crimes in Germany during the first six months of 2016," MailOnline, November 1, 2016.

82 Justin Huggler, "Merkel defiant over refugee policy: 'we can do it,'" Telegraph, August 31, 2016.

83 Nicolai Sennels, "Danish government on Muslim migrant crime: 'Worst situation since 2nd World War,'" Jihad Watch, September 17, 2017.

84 Chris Tomlinson, "Claim: Swedish Crime Stat Agency Forced to Change Findings for Political Reasons," Breitbart, December 19, 2019.

85 "Asylum Minister resigns over refugee crime report," Dutch News, May 21, 2019.

86 Ibid.

87 Ibid.

88 Ibid.

89 Ibid.

90 "German Parliament Erupts as Merkel vows to combat migrant crimes by fighting 'Right-Wing Extremists,'" RAIR Foundation USA, January 21, 2020.

91 Ibid.

92 Ibid.

93 Ibid.

94 Arthur Lyons, "Germany: Leftist officials push to import migrants amid pandemic," Voice of Europe, April 3, 2020.

95 Ivar Arpi, "It's not only Germany that covers up mass sex attacks by migrant men... Sweden's record is shameful," The Spectator, December 27, 2016; Oliver JJ Lane, "REVEALED: Full List Of 1,049 Victims, Crimes Committed During Cologne New Year's Sex Assaults," Breitbart, January 21, 2016.

96 "Cologne violence was likely planned: German justice minister," Agence France-Presse, January 10, 2016.

97 "Cologne Assaults: Police Report Outlines 'Chaotic and Shameful' New Year's Eve," Spiegel Online, January 7, 2016.

98 Ibid.

99 "New Year's Eve sex assaults also reported in Finland, Sweden and Austria," News.com.au, January 8, 2016.

100 Oliver JJ Lane, "15 Year Old Boy Was Stabbed To Death By Arab Migrant Because He Was Protecting Young Girl From Sex Assault," Breitbart, January 15, 2016.

101 Richard Orange, "Unprecedented sex harassment in Helsinki at New Year, Finnish police report," Telegraph, January 8, 2016.

102 "Opinion: Welcome to Sweden, the rape capital of the world," NA.se, February 28, 2017.

103 Michael Qazvini, "How Muslim Migration Made Malmo, Sweden A Crime Capital," Daily Wire, January 16, 2017.

104 Nicolai Sennels, "Dangerous refugees: Afghan Muslim migrants 79 times more likely to rape," Jihad Watch, July 1, 2017.

[105] Oliver JJ Lane, "Cologne Mayor: Women Should Be More Careful After Migrant Mass Rapes, Promises 'Guidance' So They Can 'Prepare,'" Breitbart, January 5, 2016.

[106] Ibid.

[107] "Flüchtling gesteht Missbrauch von Elfjähriger," Bild, February 17, 2020.

[108] Ibid.

[109] "Teenager belästigt und bedroht," Polizei Brandenburg, January 30, 2020.

[110] Nick Gutteridge, "Migrant Sex Attack 'Cover-Up': Welcome party for Cologne refugees turned into mass groping," Express, January 15, 2016.

[111] Erik Kirschbaum, "Police chief in Cologne, Germany, is fired amid criticism tied to assaults on women," Los Angeles Times, January 9, 2016.

[112] "Police tell women not to walk alone in northern Sweden," The Local, March 8, 2016.

[113] Ibid.

[114] Ibid.

[115] Helen Pidd, "Report says child sexual exploitation 'normal in parts of Greater Manchester,'" Guardian, October 30, 2014.

[116] Ibid.

[117] Ibid.

[118] Nigel Bunyan, "Rochdale grooming trial: gang convicted for sex trafficking," Telegraph, May 8, 2012.

[119] Helen Pidd, "Report says child sexual exploitation 'normal in parts of Greater Manchester.'"

[120] "Rotherham child abuse scandal: 1,400 children exploited, report finds," BBC, August 26, 2014.

[121] Ibid.

[122] Jeanette Oldham, "West Midlands Police report reveals 75 per cent of known on-street child sex groomers are Asian," BirminghamLive, October 17, 2014.

[123] Michael Buchanan, "South Yorkshire Police 'ignored Sheffield abuse claims," BBC, March 12, 2015.

[124] Lucy Thornton, "Child sex abuse gangs could have assaulted ONE MILLION youngsters in the UK," Mirror, February 5, 2015.

[125] Lizzie Dearden, "Grooming 'epidemic' as almost 19,000 children identified as sexual exploitation victims in England," Independent, December 28, 2019.

[126] Ibid.

[127] Ibid.

[128] Ibid.

[129] Jack Elsom, "Rotherham sex gang victim says police should face criminal charges for 'aiding and abetting' abuse of hundreds of children as report reveals force ignored crimes for fear of stoking racial tensions," Mailonline, January 18, 2020.

[130] Ibid.

[131] Ibid.

[132] Liam Deacon, "'Filthy' White Girls to Blame for Their Abuse, Says Wife of Muslim Groomer," Breitbart, October 1, 2017; Dale Hurd, "'Easy Meat': Britain's Muslim Rape Gang," CBN News, October 29, 2016; Lizzie Dearden, "Solicitor General calls for

longer sentences for grooming gangs who target white girls," Independent, August 12, 2017.

133 Liam Deacon, "'Filthy' White Girls to Blame for Their Abuse, Says Wife of Muslim Groomer."

134 Jordan James, "Brown Paper Envelope: Ex-PM Gordon Brown 'Let Rape Gangs Roam Free In Return For Saudi Oil Money,'" Politicalite, March 14, 2020.

135 Ibid.

136 Ibid.

137 Ibid.

138 Ibid.

139 Jack Elsom, "Rotherham sex gang victim says police should face criminal charges for 'aiding and abetting' abuse of hundreds of children as report reveals force ignored crimes for fear of stoking racial tensions," Mailonline, January 18, 2020.

140 Arj Singh, "Exclusive: Priti Patel Orders Officials To Explain Status Of Grooming Gang Review: Frustrated home secretary "being given the run around by officials" on long-awaited probe into gang ethnicity," Huffington Post, February 6, 2020.

141 Ibid.

142 Ibid.

143 Jeanette Oldham, "Birmingham City Council hid links between Asian cabbies and child sex victims for 23 years, BirminghamLive, November 24, 2014.

144 Ibid.

145 Ibid.

146 Palko Karasz, "Tommy Robinson, Anti-Muslim Activist, Is Freed on Bail in U.K.," New York Times, August 1, 2018.

147 Ibid.

148 "EXCLUSIVE: Tommy Robinson tells Ezra Levant about prison treatment, thanks supporters," Rebel Media, August 3, 2018.

149 Martin Robinson and Iain Burns, "'I'm not a victim, I'm a target': Ex-EDL leader Tommy Robinson breaks silence to say he suffered 'mental torture' in prison after 13-month jail term is quashed—as he reveals he will join family for Tenerife holiday," Mailonline, August 1, 2018.

150 "Finland: Short sentences for Muslim grooming gang who raped 12-year-old girl," Voice of Europe, April 2, 2020.

151 Eva Janssen, "Belgium: Afghan man convicted of assaulting teenage girl," Voice of Europe, February 6, 2020.

152 Ella Hill, "As a Rotherham grooming gang survivor, I want people to know about the religious extremism which inspired my abusers," Independent, March 18, 2018.

153 Federico Giuliani, "La stuprano inneggiando Allah. Poi postano il video dell'abuso sui social," Il Giornale, December 26, 2019.

154 Rukmini Callimachi, "ISIS Enshrines a Theology of Rape," New York Times, August 13, 2015.

155 Chris Tomlinson, "Morocco Police to Patrol Paris Streets to Tackle Migrant Youth Gangs," Breitbart, July 20, 2018.

156 Przemek Skwirczynski, "Polish MP: Germans Going to Great Lengths to Cover Crimes Of Their Arab Guests," *Breitbart*, July 30, 2016.

157 Liam Deacon, "Claim: Dutch Police Bribe Newspaper to Bury Data on Criminal Asylum Seekers," *Breitbart*, May 4, 2017; Donna Rachel Edmunds, "Swedish Police Stop Reporting Suspects' Ethnicity For Fear of Being Branded Racist," *Breitbart*, January 15, 2016.

158 Manasi Gopalakrishnan, "'Islamic State' reportedly training terrorists to enter Europe as asylum seekers," DW, November 14, 2016.

159 Max Fisher, "Here is ISIS's statement claiming responsibility for the Paris attacks," Vox, November 14, 2015.

160 Ben Norton, "Our terrorism double standard: After Paris, let's stop blaming Muslims and take a hard look at ourselves," Salon.com, November 15, 2015; Chauncey DeVega, "And so the hate speech begins: Let Paris be the end of the right's violent language toward activists," Salon.com, November 14, 2015.

161 Natalie Nougayrède, "Paris attacks leave France in trauma, fearing for the future," Guardian, November 13, 2015.

162 "Don't link Paris attacks to migrant influx: German interior minister," AFP, November 14, 2015.

163 Jacob Bojesson, "German Intel Agency Says Hundreds of Jihadis Arrived Among Refugees," *Daily Caller*, July 5, 2017.

164 "At least two dead, 11 wounded in Strasbourg shooting," RTÉ, December 4, 2018.

165 "Inevitable threat? Strasbourg gunman was on terror watch list, had grenades at home," RT, December 11, 2018.

166 Ibid.

167 Ed Riley, "'We CANNOT watch them all': Scotland Yark [sic] anti-terror chief Neil Basu says officers don't have resources to watch every 3,000 extremist suspects," Mailonline, February 5, 2020.

168 Ibid.

169 Abū Muhammad al-'Adnānī ash-Shāmī, "Indeed Your Lord Is Ever Watchful," September 21, 2014.

170 Ibid.

171 Ibid.

172 Ibid.

173 Ibid.

174 Ibid.

175 Ibid.

176 Ibid.

177 Ibid.

178 Ambrose Evans-Pritchard, "Ex-Hezbollah charged with inciting rioting," *London Daily Telegraph*, November 30, 2002.

179 Omer Taspinar, "Europe's Muslim Street," *Muslim News*, March 11, 2003.

180 Andrew Morse and Richard Gizbert, "Opposite Sides: Anti-Semitic Violence Erupts in France, Amid Mideast Conflict," *ABCNews.com*, April 3, 2002.

181 Christopher Caldwell, "Allah Mode: France's Islam problem," Weekly Standard, July 15, 2002.

182 "Rabbi stabbed at Paris synagogue," BBC, January 4, 2003.

183 Craig S. Smith, "French Jews Tell of a New and Threatening Wave of Anti-Semitism," New York Times, March 22, 2003.

184 "Copenhagen imam accused of calling for killing of Jews," BBC, May 11, 2017.

185 Imam Muslim, Sahih Muslim, Abdul Hamid Siddiqi, translator, Kitab Bhavan, revised edition 2000, no. 6985.

186 "Copenhagen imam accused of calling for killing of Jews."

187 Ibid.

188 "Imam prædiker om jødedrab:—Jeg tror ikke, han mener noget ondt med det," Nyheder, May 11, 2017.

189 Ibid.

190 Ibid.

191 "Copenhagen imam accused of calling for killing of Jews."

192 Giulio Meotti, "Disappearing Jewish Symbol Reveals Europe's Submission to Islam," The Geller Report, March 1, 2017.

193 Simon Kent, "Jewish Student Driven Out of Berlin School by Threats and Violence from Muslim Classmates," Breitbart, May 28, 2017.

194 Ibid.

195 Ibid.

196 Ibid.

197 Ibid.

198 Giulio Meotti, "Disappearing Jewish Symbol Reveals Europe's Submission to Islam.".

199 "French intellectuals accuse authorities of covering up Jewish woman's slaying by Muslim neighbor," JTA, June 9, 2017.

200 Ibid.

201 Ibid.

202 Harvey Day, "Man is held by police in north London after roaming through heavily Jewish area shouting 'Allah Allah' and 'I'm going to kill you all,'" Mailonline, June 8, 2017.

203 Ibid.

204 Souad Mekhennet and Adam Goldman, "'Jihadi John': Islamic State killer is identified as Londoner Mohammed Emwazi," Washington Post, February 26, 2015; "'Jihadi John' named as Mohammed Emwazi from London," BBC, February 26, 2015.

205 "'Jihadi John' named as Mohammed Emwazi from London," BBC, February 26, 2015.

206 Ibid.

207 Robert Verkaik, "'Three runaway teen 'jihadi brides' feared to be heading into the clutches of British women leading ISIS religious police who dole out savage beatings," MailOnline, February 25, 2015; Harriet Sherwood, Sandra Laville, Kim Willsher, Ben Knight, Maddy French and Lauren Gambino, "Schoolgirl jihadis: the female Islamists leaving home to join Isis fighters," Guardian, September 29, 2014.

[208] Harriet Sherwood, Sandra Laville, Kim Willsher, Ben Knight, Maddy French and Lauren Gambino, "Schoolgirl jihadis: the female Islamists leaving home to join Isis fighters."

[209] Ibid.

[210] Ibid.

[211] Harriet Sherwood, Sandra Laville, Kim Willsher, Ben Knight, Maddy French and Lauren Gambino, "Schoolgirl jihadis: the female Islamists leaving home to join Isis fighters," Guardian, September 29, 2014.

[212] Jake Wallis Simons and Chris Greenwood, "EXCLUSIVE: Father who blamed police for not stopping his daughter joining ISIS attended 2012 rally led by hate preacher Anjem Choudary and attended by Lee Rigby killer," Daily Mail, March 26, 2015.

[213] Robert Verkaik, "'Three runaway teen 'jihadi brides' feared to be heading into the clutches of British women leading ISIS religious police who dole out savage beatings," MailOnline, February 25, 2015.

[214] Robert Verkaik, "'Three runaway teen 'jihadi brides' feared to be heading into the clutches of British women leading ISIS religious police who dole out savage beatings," MailOnline, February 25, 2015.

[215] Ibid.

[216] Ibid.

[217] Ibid.

[218] Ibid.

[219] Ibid.

[220] Ashley Fantz and Atika Schubert, "From Scottish teen to ISIS bride and recruiter: the Aqsa Mahmood story," CNN, February 24, 2015; Harriet Sherwood, Sandra Laville, Kim Willsher, Ben Knight, Maddy French and Lauren Gambino, "Schoolgirl jihadis: the female Islamists leaving home to join Isis fighters."

[221] Oussama Cherribi, "Imams and Issues: The Politics of Islam in European Public Space," presentation at the American Political Science Association, San Francisco, California, August 30-September 2, 2001.

[222] Ibid.

[223] Hani Ramadan, "La charia incomprise," LeMonde, September 10, 2002.

[224] John L. Allen, Jr., "Europe's Muslims worry bishops," National Catholic Reporter, October 22, 1999.

[225] Liam Deacon, "UK: Whites Scared, White-Owned Businesses Stoned in a Racially Divided Bradford 'Heading for Disaster'" Breitbart, December 24, 2017.

[226] Akbar Ahmed, "Italy must remember its pluralist past," Daily Times, March 31, 2018.

[227] Edward Gibbon, *The History of the Decline and Fall of the Roman Empire*, vol. 5, ch. 52, part 4, 327.

[228] Akbar Ahmed, "Abdur Rahman I: The beginning of the glory of Muslim Spain," Daily Times, June 16, 2018.

[229] Kenneth Baxter Wolf, *Christian Martyrs in Muslim Spain,* Cambridge University Press, 1988, p. 12.

[230] Ibid.

231 Ibid., p. 34.

232 Darío Fernández-Morera, *The Myth of the Andalusian Paradise*, ISI Books, 2016, p. 159.

233 "World War II graves smashed in Libya," Al Jazeera, March 5, 2012; "Insult to WWII heroes: Graves of British troops smashed and desecrated by Libyan Islamists in protest over U.S. soldiers' Koran burning," Daily Mail, March 2, 2012.

234 V. S. Naipaul, *Among the Believers: An Islamic Journey*, Vintage Books, 1982, pp. 141–2.

235 Ibid.

236 Ibid, p. 65.

237 Raymond Ibrahim, "Video: 'I Hate Christians and Am Disgusted by Them'— Muslim Cleric," RaymondIbrahim.com, April 1, 2013.

238 V. S. Naipaul, *Among the Believers*, p. 18.

239 Philip Mansel, *Constantinople: City of the World's Desire 1453–1924*, St. Martin's Griffin, 1998, p. 437.

240 Aid to the Church in Need, "Religious Freedom in the Majority Islamic Countries 1998 Report: Turkey."

241 Aid to the Church in Need, "Religious Freedom in the Majority Islamic Countries 1998 Report: Cyprus."

242 Aid to the Church in Need, "Religious Freedom in the Majority Islamic Countries 1998 Report: Tunisia."

243 Sayyid Qutb, *Milestones*, The Mother Mosque Foundation, n.d., pp. 10–11.

244 Laura Clark, "Teachers drop the Holocaust to avoid offending Muslims," *Daily Mail*, April 2, 2007.

245 Jamie Pyatt, "Jail loos turned from East," *The Sun*, January 31, 2007.

246 Stuart MacDonald, "Sniffer dogs to wear 'Muslim' bootees," *Times* of London, July 6, 2008.

247 "Piggy banks 'offend UK Muslims,'" AAP, October 24, 2005.

248 Nick Britten, "Schoolboys disciplined for 'refusing to pray to Allah,'" Telegraph, July 5, 2008.

249 Natasha Courtenay-Smith, "How can my son be racist, asks mother of Down's boy charged after playground spat with Asian girl," Daily Mail, April 17, 2008.

250 "Muslim council chiefs ban ALL members from 'tea and sandwiches' in meetings which take place during Ramadan," Evening Standard, August 28, 2008.

251 "'Allahu Akbar' echoes across Britain as BBC broadcasts 'Azaan' for the first time," Global Village Space, April 15, 2020.

252 Ibid.

253 Ibid.

254 Ibid.

255 Jules Gomes, "Muslim Declares Muhammad's Supremacy Over Jesus at Catholic Mass," Church Militant, April 3, 2020.

256 "Last words of a terrorist," Guardian, September 30, 2001.

257 Mark Hookham, "Fury as primary school tells pupils to say 'Baby Boy Jesus' instead of 'Lord Jesus' while singing Away In A Manger so that pupils of all faiths can join in," The Mail on Sunday, December 14, 2019.

258 Ibid.

259 Ibid.

260 Ibid.

261 Nick Enoch and Rachael Burford, "Two arrested over Facebook and YouTube video of Koran burning amid spate of race attacks in wake of London and Manchester terror attacks," Mailonline, June 8, 2017.

262 "London attackers' fake suicide belts revealed," Sky News, June 11, 2017.

263 Frances Gibb, "Case dismissed: Lord Chief Justice lays down law on Sharia," Times of London, July 4, 2008.

264 Christopher Hope and James Kirkup, "Muslims in Britain should be able to live under sharia, says top judge," Daily Mail, July 4, 2008.

265 Ibid.

266 Frances Gibb, "Case dismissed."

267 Christopher Hope and James Kirkup, "Muslims in Britain should be able to live under sharia, says top judge."

268 "Sharia law in UK is 'unavoidable," BBC, February 7, 2008.

269 "British Muslim women abused under Sharia courts—report," Christian Institute, March 27, 2015.

270 Ibid.

271 Hannah Summers, "Sharia courts review branded a 'whitewash' over appointment 'bias' concerns," Independent, July 9, 2016.

272 Leda Reynolds, "Sharia court told rape victim to RETURN to her attacker husband," Express, November 14, 2016.

273 Ibid.

274 Ibid.

275 Ibid.

276 Ibid.

277 Natalie Corner, "The moment a Muslim mother is forced to ask the permission of Islamic clerics in a BRITISH Sharia court to divorce her drug dealer husband," Daily Mail, March 2, 2017.

278 Eva Cahen, "Report Records 'Explosion' of Anti-Semitic Violence in France," CNSNews.com, March 28, 2003.

279 Elizabeth Bryant, "Fallaci goes on trial for anti-Muslim book," United Press International, October 9, 2002.

280 "Bardot Fined Over Racial Hatred," BBC, June 3, 2008.

281 "The Many Faces of Islam," Time Europe, December 16, 2002.

282 "Egyptian volunteers line up to fight in Iraq," Agence France-Press, April 8, 2003.

283 Christopher Caldwell, "Allah Mode."

284 Christopher Caldwell, "Allah Mode Part 2," Weekly Standard, July 6, 2002.

[285] Kim Housego, "France May Expel Islamic Extremists," Associated Press, April 16, 2003.

[286] Elaine Sciolino, "French Threaten Expulsions After Islam Radical Victory," New York Times, April 16, 2003.

[287] Christopher Caldwell, "Allah Mode."

[288] Hugh Schofield, "France's Islamic heartland," BBC, April 18, 2003.

[289] Kim Housego, "France May Expel Islamic Extremists," Associated Press, April 16, 2003.

[290] Elaine Sciolino, "French Threaten Expulsions."

[291] Ibid.

[292] Lorenzo Vidino, "Emmanuel Macron's War on Islamism Is Europe's Future," Foreign Policy, February 24, 2020.

[293] "Question: Qu'est-ce que vous pensez de la polygamie?" www.sarkozy.fr, March 26, 2007..

[294] "Youths in France continue to riot over Sarkozy victory," Reuters, May 8, 2007.

[295] "Sarkozy call to help minorities," BBC, December 29, 2005.

[296] "Sarkozy voices 'support' for Dutch PM in anti-Islam film row," Expatica, March 6, 2008.

[297] "Muslims condemn Dutch lawmaker's film," CNN, March 28, 2008.

[298] Rukmini Callimachi, "Defame Islam, Get Sued?" Associated Press, March 14, 2008.

[299] Ibid.

[300] "Muslims condemn Dutch lawmaker's film," CNN, March 28, 2008.

[301] Ekmeleddin Ihsanoglu, "Speech of Secretary General at the thirty-fifth session of the Council of Foreign Ministers of the Organisation of the Islamic Conference," June 18, 2008.

[302] Alexis Amory, "Islamofascism Rising in Holland," FrontPage Magazine, March 6, 2003; Marlise Simons, "Belgium's Malcolm X: Immigrant activist sets out to 'rock the boat,'" New York Times, March 5, 2003.

[303] Jennifer Ehrlich and Tom Vandyck, "'Belgian Malcolm X' seeks office," Christian Science Monitor, May 16, 2003.

[304] Dyab Abou Jahjah, "Our Own Agenda: Is the Arab world Europe's nemesis, or its last hope?" Al-Ahram Weekly, September 12, 2002.

[305] Arab European League, "Vision and Philosophy," http://www.arabeuropean.org/aboutus.html.

[306] Ibid.

[307] Marlise Simons, "Belgium's Malcolm X."

[308] John Miller, "The Activist," in "The Many Faces of Islam," Time Europe, December 16, 2002.

[309] Ambrose Evans-Pritchard, "Ex-Hezbollah charged with inciting rioting," London Daily Telegraph, November 30, 2002.

[310] Ibid.

[311] Alexis Amory, "Islamofascism."

[312] Ihsan Tharoor, "Europe's fear of Muslim refugees echoes rhetoric of 1930s antisemitism," Washington Post, September 2, 2015.

[313] "Sveriges kulturarvschef Qaisar Mahmood: 'Jag har inte läst något om kulturarv,'" Samhällsnytt, February 2, 2018.

[314] "Jag kämpar för att bli svensk," Svenska Dagbladet, February 4, 2012.

[315] "Sveriges kulturarvschef Qaisar Mahmood: 'Jag har inte läst något om kulturarv.'".

[316] Tim Collins, "Were Vikings influenced by ISLAM? Arabic embroidery bearing the name 'Allah' is uncovered on 10th Century Norse burial clothes," Mailonline, October 12, 2017.

[317] Lucy Pasha-Robinson, "Viking textile did not feature word 'Allah', expert says," Independent, October 17, 2017.

[318] George Gurley, "The Rage of Oriana Fallaci," Observer, January 27, 2003.

[319] Oriana Fallaci, "An Interview with Khomeini," *New York Times*, October 7, 1979.

[320] Ibid.

[321] Margaret Talbot, "The Agitator: Oriana Fallaci Directs Her Fury toward Islam," *New Yorker*, June 5, 2006.

[322] Ibid.

[323] Oriana Fallaci, *The Force of Reason*, Rizzoli, 2006, p. 269.

[324] "Italian Judge Bans Crucifix From School," Associated Press, October 27, 2003.

[325] "Paper: Italian Church Attack Plotted," Associated Press, June 23, 2002.

[326] "Muslim Activist Sues Pope, Cardinal," Associated Press, February 29, 2004.

[327] "Fallaci To Go On Trial For Defaming Islam," AGI, May 24, 2005.

[328] "Italian Author To Face Charges Of Defaming Islam," Reuters, May 25, 2005.

[329] Tunku Varadarajan, "Prophet of Decline," Wall Street Journal, June 23, 2005.

[330] Ibid.

[331] "Fallaci, processo aggiornato a dicembre," L'Eco di Bergamo, June 25, 2006.

[332] Liz McGregor and John Hooper, "Oriana Fallaci," Guardian, September 15, 2006.

[333] Chris Allen, *Islamophobia*, Ashgate Publishing, Ltd., 2013, p. 175.

[334] Bruno Cousin and Tommaso Vitale, "Italian Intellectuals and the Promotion of Islamophobia After 9/11," in *Global Islamophobia: Muslims and Moral Panic in the West*, George Morgan and Scott Poynting, editors, Ashgate Publishing, Ltd., 2013, chapter 3.

[335] "Rome nixes naming street after journalist Fallaci, citing past statements on Islam," Haaretz, September 17, 2014.

[336] Christopher Hitchens, "Holy Writ," The Atlantic, April 2003.

[337] Oriana Fallaci, *The Force of Reason*, pp. 56–57.

[338] Oriana Fallaci, *The Force of Reason*, p. 53.

[339] Tunku Varadarajan, "Prophet of Decline," Wall Street Journal, June 23, 2005.

[340] Hannah Roberts, "ISIS threatens to send 500,000 migrants to Europe as a 'psychological weapon' in chilling echo of Gaddafi's prophecy that the Mediterranean 'will become a sea of chaos," Mailonline, February 18, 2015.

[341] Jack Blanchard, "Officials warn 20,000 ISIS jihadis 'have infiltrated Syrian refugee camps,'" Mirror, September 14, 2015.

342 Ian Drury, "Four out of five migrants are NOT from Syria: EU figures expose the 'lie' that the majority of refugees are fleeing war zone," Daily Mail, September 18, 2015.

343 Chris Tomlinson, "Marion Marechal Calls for French to Resist 'Great Replacement,'" Breitbart, October 1, 2019.

344 Alice Philipson, "Italians Outraged After Headmaster Scraps Christmas Carol Concert following Paris Attacks," Telegraph, November 29, 2015.

345 Virginia Hale, "Christians Told to 'Pray In Silence . . . Don't Disturb the Migrants,'" Breitbart, June 6, 2016.

346 Chris Tomlinson, "Spanish Court Orders Pension Payments to Moroccan Polygamist's Two Widows," Breitbart, January 25, 2020.

347 "Disney's Piglet Banned in Middle East!" QatarLiving.com, January 28, 2007.

348 "Pigs' Faces BlackenedOout in Papers in Malaysia," AFP, January 21, 2014.

349 "Swiss Muslims File Suit Over 'Racist' Fallaci Book," Islam Online, June 20, 2002.

350 Ibid.

351 Ibid.

352 Oriana Fallaci, The Force of Reason, p. 195.

353 Ibid., pp. 195–196.

354 Isabel Hunter, "EXCLUSIVE—'Let down by the Pope on Lesbos': Christian brother and sister told they would be rescued by Holy Father then left behind over EU deal to send migrants to Turkey," Mailonline, April 22, 2016.

355 Andrew Osborn, "'I Shot Fortuyn for Dutch Muslims,' Says Accused," Guardian, March 28, 2003.

356 Toby Sterling, "Dutch Filmmaker Theo Van Gogh Murdered," Associated Press, November 2, 2004.

357 "Slaughter and 'Submission,'" CBS News, August 20, 2006.

358 "Ayaan Hirsi Ali: My Life under a Fatwa," Independent, November 26, 2007.

359 Sterling, "Dutch Filmmaker."

360 Philippe Naughton, "Van Gogh Killer Jailed for Life," Times Online, July 26, 2005.

361 "Ayaan Hirsi Ali."

362 "Prison Gives Van Gogh's Killer Ultra-Orthodox Islam Books," NIS News, May 14, 2007.

363 "Dutch Filmmaker Killed, Muslims Condemn," IslamOnline.net, November 2, 2004.

364 Lucia Kubosova, "Brussels Defends Pope's Freedom of Expression," EU Observer, September 18, 2006.

365 Soeren Kern, "'A Black Day for Austria,'" Gatestone Institute, December 26, 2011.

366 Muhammed Ibn Ismaiel Al-Bukhari, Sahih al-Bukhari: The Translation of the Meanings, translated by Muhammad M. Khan, Darussalam, 1997, vol. 5, book 63, no. 3896; cf. Bukhari, vol. 7, book 67, no. 5158.

367 Sahih al-Bukhari, vol. 5, book 63, no. 3894.

368 Soeren Kern, "'A Black Day for Austria.'"

369 Ibid.

370 Ibid.

371 Ibid.

372 "Next Stop: The European Court of Human Rights," Gates of Vienna, December 11, 2013.

373 Soeren Kern, "'A Black Day for Austria.'"

374 Soeren Kern, "Free Speech Found Guilty by Europe," Gatestone Institute, April 23, 2012.

375 Soeren Kern, "Free Speech Found Guilty."

376 Ibid.

377 "Bardot Fined Over Racial Hatred," BBC News, June 3, 2008.

378 Giulio Meotti, "Western Publishers Submit to Islam," Gatestsone Institute, September 11, 2016.

379 Soeren Kern, "Free Speech Found Guilty."

380 Ibid.

381 Ibid.

382 Ibid.

383 Giulio Meotti, "Western Publishers Submit to Islam.".

384 Ibid.

385 Tulay Karadeniz and Gabriela Baczynska, "To Europe's chagrin, Turkey digs in its heels on terrorism law," Reuters, May 11, 2016.

386 Ibid.

387 Ibid.

388 "Turkish Leader Erdogan Assails Europe, Calls It 'Sick,' 'Collapsing,'" Radio Free Europe/Radio Liberty, April 10, 2017.

389 Ibid.

390 Vincent Wood, "EU leaders 'TERRIFIED Turkey could TURN ITS BACK on controversial migrant deal'" Express, April 18, 2017.

391 Ibid.

392 Ibid.

393 Lizzie Dearden, "Recep Tayyip Erdogan: EU ruling on headscarf bans starts 'clash between Islam and Christianity,'" Independent, March 16, 2017.

394 "Erdogan warns Austria imam crackdown will lead to holy war," AFP, June 10, 2018.

395 Jack Montgomery, "Turkey Orders EU to Submit or 'We Open Gates and Send 3.6m Refugees,'" Breitbart, October 11, 2019.

396 Chris Tomlinson, "Turkey's Islamist President Makes Fresh Threat to Flood Europe with Migrants" Breitbart, November 10, 2019.

397 Chris Tomlinson, "Erdogan Opens the Gates: Syrian Migrants Granted Unhindered Passage to Europe," Breitbart, February 27, 2020.

398 Ibid.

399 Ibid.

400 "Erdogan warns 'millions' of refugees will soon head toward Europe," Ekathimerini, March 2, 2020.

401 Jack Montgomery, "WATCH: Turkey Arms Migrants with Tear Gas, Sends Freed Prisoners to Border, Claims Greek Government," Breitbart, March 6, 2020.

402 Ibid.

403 Ibid.

404 Ibid.

405 Chris Tomlinson, "Erdogan to Hold Migrant Summit With Macron and Merkel in Istanbul," Breitbart, March 12, 2020.

406 Ibid.

407 Ibid.

408 Jack Montgomery, "Turkey Orders EU to Submit or 'We Open Gates and Send 3.6m Refugees,'" Breitbart, October 11, 2019.

409 Arthur Lyons, "EU to fork over another €500 million to the Turkish regime to stop migrants," Voice of Europe, March 8, 2020.

410 Ibid.

411 Chris Tomlinson, "Large Number of North Africans Among Migrants on Greek Border," Breitbart, March 10, 2020.

412 Chris Tomlinson, "Turkey: Migrants Will Return to Border After Coronavirus Outbreak Ends," Breitbart, March 31, 2020.

413 Ibid.

414 "Turkey's Erdogan blinks; pulls his migrant army back from Greek border amid virus pandemic," Associated Press, March 28, 2020.

415 Chris Tomlinson, "Turkey: Migrants Will Return to Border."

416 "Turkey's Erdogan blinks."

417 Ibid.

418 Ibid.

419 Chris Tomlinson, "Turkey: Migrants Will Return to Border.".

420 Fabian Eberhard, "Erdogan warnt Türken in der Schweiz vor Integration," Blick, December 22, 2019.

421 Özlem Gezer and Anna Reimann, "Erdogan Urges Turks Not to Assimilate," Spiegel Online, February 28, 2011.

422 Ibid.

423 Ibid.

424 Ibid.

425 Ibid.

426 Fabian Eberhard, "Erdogan warnt Türken in der Schweiz vor Integration," Blick, December 22, 2019.

427 Ibid.

428 David Frum, "The Real Lesson of My Debate With Steve Bannon," The Atlantic, November 4, 2018.

429 Louisa Wright, "German state fights Islamist extremism with YouTube satire," DW, August 25, 2019.

430 Ibid.

[431] "Europe's far-right leaders raise voices against migration and Islam ahead of EU vote," Associated Press, April 25, 2019.

[432] Ibid.

[433] Ibid.

[434] Ibid.

[435] Kirsty Lang, "Pim Fortuyn: Maverick Dutch rightwinger poised for success," Guardian, May 8, 2002.

[436] Charles Paul Freund, "Fortuyn's Folly: How an assassinated Dutch politician frustrated journalists," Reason, May 7, 2002.

[437] John Hooper, "More to Fortuyn than anti-immigrant populist," Guardian, May 8, 2002; Andrew Osborn, "'I shot Fortuyn for Dutch Muslims,' says accused."

[438] Ibid.

[439] Kirsty Lang, "Pim Fortuyn."

[440] Andrew Osborn, "'I shot Fortuyn for Dutch Muslims,' says accused."

[441] Ibid.

[442] "Fortuyn killer now has doubts," Associated Press, March 31, 2003.

[443] "Dutch politician's killer gets 18 years," *London Evening Standard*, April 15, 2003.

[444] Pierre-Antoine Souchard, "Mayor of Paris stabbed," Associated Press, October 7, 2002.

[445] Abigail Levene, "Anti-gay talk sparks Dutch outcry," Reuters, May 10, 2001.

[446] "Islam Film Dutch MP to Be Charged," BBC, January 21, 2009.

[447] Ibid.

[448] Ibid.

[449] "Mixed Reactions to Wilders Court Decision," DutchNews.nl, January 21, 2009.

[450] Hillel Fendel, "Geert Wilders to INN: 'Traditional European Freedom at Stake,'" Israel National News, September 2, 2010.

[451] Patrick Goodenough, "Anti-Islam Dutch Lawmaker Says He's Being Denied a Fair Trial; Court Rejects Most of His Witness List," CNS News, February 4, 2010; Robert Spencer, "Dutch Court Railroading Wilders: Disallows All but Three of His Witnesses," Jihad Watch, February 3, 2010.

[452] "Geert Wilders Cleared of Hate Charges by Dutch Court," BBC, June 23, 2011.

[453] Ibid.

[454] Toby Sterling and Anthony Deutsch, "Dutch Far Right Leader Geert Wilders on Trial for Discrimination," Reuters, March 18, 2016.

[455] Sofia Lotto Persio, "Anti-Islam Politician Geert Wilders Found Guilty of Inciting Discrimination in Hate Speech Trial," International Business Times, December 9, 2016.

[456] Robert Spencer, "Geert Wilders Puts the Political Elites on Notice," FrontPage Magazine, June 11, 2018.

[457] Robert Spencer, "Britain Capitulates to Jihad," FrontPage Magazine, June 26, 2013.

[458] Jamie Doward, "Muslim cleric banned in Pakistan is preaching in UK mosques," Observer, December 17, 2016.

459 Raheem Kassam, "'Behead, Burn, And Crush Gays' Islamic Preacher To Deliver 10 Days Of Lectures In London," Breitbart, October 4, 2016.

460 Iram Ramzan, "Clerics who hailed killer at mosque," Oldham Evening Chronicle, August 16, 2016.

461 Tom Porter, "Pakistani 'hate preacher' who glorifies Islamist murder welcomed by Archbishop of Canterbury," International Business Times, July 21, 2016.

462 Caroline Wheeler, "Britain BANS heroic bishops: Persecuted Christian leaders from war zones refused entry," Express, December 4, 2016.

463 Robert Spencer, "Geert Wilders Puts the Political Elites on Notice," FrontPage Magazine, June 11, 2018.

464 Ibid.

465 Aurelien Breeden, "French Court Acquits Marine Le Pen of Hate Speech," New York Times, December 15, 2015.

466 Ibid.

467 Ben McPartland, "Marine Le Pen furious after being ordered to undergo psychiatric tests," The Local, September 20, 2018.

468 Ibid.

469 Ibid.

470 Ibid.

471 Ibid.

472 Ibid.

473 Chris Tomlinson, "Le Pen Triumphs Over Macron in EU Election Exit Poll, Calls for Fresh National Elections," Breitbart, May 26, 2019.

474 Ibid.

475 "Soros and EU striving for 'mixed, Muslimized Europe', says Hungarian PM Orban," RT, July 23, 2017.

476 Ibid.

477 Jack Montgomery, "WATCH: Hungary Vows to 'Shake Up' EU in Ad Taking Aim at Migrant Crime, Terrorism, Open Borders," Breitbart, October 13, 2018.

478 Ibid.

479 Ibid.

480 Ross Ibbetson, "Viktor Orban warns Hungary will 'use force' to fend off a new wave of migrants if Turkey delivers on its threat to allow refugees to flood into Europe," Mailonline, October 17, 2019.

481 Ibid.

482 Thomas D. Williams, "Viktor Orban: Matteo Salvini Is 'My Hero,'" Breitbart, August 28, 2018.

483 Ibid.

484 Ibid.

485 Ibid.

486 Ibid.

487 Chris Tomlinson, "Salvini Demands Security Services Increase Observation of Islamic Cultural Centres," Breitbart, April 26, 2019.

[488] Ibid.

[489] Thomas D. Williams, "Viktor Orban: Matteo Salvini Is 'My Hero.'"

[490] Virginia Hale, "Commission: EU Must Curb National Sovereignty to Kill Populism," Breitbart, September 27, 2018.

[491] Ibid.

[492] Victoria Friedman, "Top Eurocrat Juncker Attacks 'Stupid Populists' in Attempts to Reach out to Eurosceptics," Breitbart, October 9, 2018.

[493] Ibid.

[494] Ibid.

[495] Ibid.

[496] Thomas D. Williams, "Vatican Expresses Concerns Over 'Spread of Nationalism, Populism,'" Breitbart, February 14, 2017.

[497] Ibid.

[498] Ibid.

[499] Ibid.

[500] Ibid.

[501] Thomas D. Williams, "Pope Francis Compares Populists to Hitler, Born of 'Hate,'" Breitbart, October 25, 2018.

[502] Ibid.

[503] Ibid.

[504] Ibid.

[505] Ibid.

[506] Ibid.

[507] Virginia Hale, "Merkel Bashes Populists, Calls for 'Pro-Minority' Europe of 'Values' Ahead of Elections," Breitbart, May 21, 2019.

[508] Ibid.

[509] Ibid.

[510] Ibid.

[511] Ibid.

[512] Krisztina Than and Gergely Szakacs, "Hungary's strongman Viktor Orban wins third term in power," Reuters, April 8, 2018.

[513] Krisztina Than and Marton Dunai, "Hungary's Fidesz wins 52% of vote; Orban vows to halt immigration," Reuters, May 26, 2019.

[514] Ibid.

[515] Jack Montgomery, "Populist Revolt Spreads: Estonia's New Govt Ministers Will Oppose EU Integration," Breitbart, May 20, 2019.

[516] Virginia Hale, "Macron Vows Punishment for States Refusing Third World Migration," Breitbart, September 21, 2018.

[517] Ibid.

[518] Ibid.

[519] Victoria Friedman, "Hungary Vows It Will Protect Europe from Illegal Mass Migration, Again," Breitbart, March 5, 2020.

[520] Ibid.

[521] Damon Johnston, "WTC Survivor's Son Leaves NY To Fight With Taliban," The Courier Mail, November 7, 2001.

[522] Sayyid Qutb, "A Muslim's Nationality and His Belief."

[523] Ibid.

[524] Christopher Caldwell, "Allah Mode."

[525] Tariq Ramadan, *To Be a European Muslim: A Study of Islamic Sources in the European Context*, The Islamic Foundation, 1999. P. 165.

[526] Tariq Ramadan, p. 172.

[527] Xavier Ternisien, "Le 'double langage' de Tariq Ramadan en procès à Lyon," Le Monde, September 27, 2002.

[528] "Islamic Scholar Tariq Ramadan, after Serving Time for Rape Charges: The French Judicial System Imprisoned Me as Part of a Political Plot to Destroy My Reputation; This Can Happen to Any Vocal Muslim," Middle East Media Research Institute, December 20, 2019.

[529] Ibid.

[530] Ibid.

[531] "Tariq Ramadan formally charged with two more counts of rape," RFI, February 13, 2020.

[532] "Swiss woman files rape complaint against Islamic scholar," Reuters, April 13, 2018.

[533] "French Activist Henda Ayari on Her Salafi Past, Alleged Rape by Tariq Ramadan, and Struggle to Help Women Who Fell Prey to Extremists," Middle East Media Research Institute, April 7, 2018.

[534] Caroline Fourest, *Brother Tariq: The Doublespeak of Tariq Ramadan*, Encounter Books, 2008, p. 368.

[535] Ibid.

[536] Ibid.

[537] Caroline Fourest, "La double vie de Tariq Ramadan," Marianne, October 27, 2017.

[538] Ibid.

[539] Paul Donnelly, "Tariq Ramadan: The Muslim Martin Luther?" *Salon.com*, February 15, 2002.

[540] Xavier Ternisien, "Le 'double langage' de Tariq Ramadan en procès à Lyon."

[541] Tariq Ramadan, p. 173.

[542] Tariq Ramadan, p. 176.

[543] Sami A. Aldeeb Abu-Sahlieh, *Muslims in the West: Redefining the Separation of Church and State*, translated by Sheldon Lee Gosline, Shangri-La Publications, 2002. P. 96.

[544] Ibid.

[545] Joseph Algazy, "'My fellow Muslims, we must fight anti-Semitism,'" Haaretz, May 26, 2002.

[546] Tariq Ramadan, "Foreword," in Hassan al-Banna, *Al-Ma'thurat*, Awakening Publications, 2001.

[547] Ibid.

548 Hasan al-Banna, "On Jihad," in *Five Tracts of Hasan al-Banna*, translated by Charles Wendell, Berkeley, 1978, pp. 142, 150, 154.

549 Ibid.

550 Ibid.

551 Tariq Ramadan, *To Be a European Muslim.*

552 Ayub Khan, "Muslim Philosopher Addresses Islam and the West," Islam Online, April 6, 2002.

553 Martin Kramer, *Ivory Towers on Sand: The Failure of Middle Eastern Studies in America*, Washington Institute for Near East Policy, 2001, p. 54.

554 Aaron Brown, "'Just wait...' Islamic State reveals it has smuggled THOUSANDS of extremists into Europe," Express, November 18, 2015.

555 Ibid.

556 Ibid.

557 Charlie Spiering, "National Intelligence Director Clapper: Islamic State Exploiting Migrant Crisis In Europe," Breitbart, April 25, 2016.

558 "Former Jordanian Minister Ali Al-Faqir Vows to Conquer Spain and Rome and Declares: America and the EU Will Soon Come to an End," Middle East Media Research Institute (MEMRI), May 2, 2008.

559 "Hamas MP and Cleric Yunis Al-Astal in a Friday Sermon: We Will Conquer Rome, and from There Continue to Conquer the Two Americas and Eastern Europe," Middle East Media Research Institute (MEMRI), April 11, 2008.

560 "Foreign ISIS Fighter in Iraq: We Will Conquer Jerusalem, Rome, and Spain," Middle East Media Research Institute (MEMRI), May 17, 2014.

561 "Canada Friday Sermon by Imam Shaban Sherif Mady: Rome Will Be Conquered like Constantinople Was," Middle East Media Research Institute (MEMRI), February 16, 2016.

562 "Leading Sunni Sheikh Yousef Al-Qaradhawi and Other Sheikhs Herald the Coming Conquest of Rome," Middle East Media Research Institute (MEMRI), December 6, 2002.

563 Sahih Muslim 6930.

564 Abū Muhammad al-'Adnānī ash-Shāmī, "Indeed Your Lord Is Ever Watchful."

565 Adam Taylor, "The Islamic State threatens to come to Rome; Italians respond with travel advice," Washington Post, February 20, 2015.

566 "Rome prefect demands 'clear stand' from Islamic community," ANSA, November 19, 2015.

567 "Danish church defaced with Arabic graffiti saying 'We conquer Denmark," Voice of Europe, April 17, 2020.

568 Islamic State, *Black Flags from Rome (Europe)*, 2015, p. 3.

569 Ibid., pp. 3, 28.

570 Ibid., p. 28.

571 Ibid., p. 3.

572 Ibid., p. 8.

573 Ibid., p. 10.

574 Ibid., p. 14.

[575] Ibid.

[576] Ibid., p. 15.

[577] Ibid.

[578] Ibid., p. 20.

[579] Ibid., p. 21.

[580] Ibid.

[581] Ibid., p. 23.

[582] Ibid., p. 25.

[583] Ibid.

[584] Ibid., p. 28.

[585] Ibid., p. 26.

[586] Ibid., p. 35.

[587] Ibid., p. 39.

[588] Ibid., p. 45.

[589] Ibid., p. 46.

[590] Ibid., p. 64.

[591] Ibid., p. 68.

[592] "Handwritten ISIS notes 'in front of Rome, Milan monuments,'" ANSA, April 28, 2015.

[593] Islamic State, *Black Flags from Rome (Europe)*, p. 4.

[594] Imam Muslim, *Sahih Muslim*, Abdul Hamid Siddiqi, trans., Kitab Bhavan, revised edition 2000, book 41, no. 6924.

[595] Islamic State, *Black Flags from Rome (Europe)*, p. 81.

[596] Ibid.

[597] "90 percent said they would convert to Islam if the IS came—generation without ideals," Jihad Watch, April 20, 2016, translated from "90 Prozent würden zum Islam konvertieren, wenn der IS käme—Generation ohne Ideale," Katholisches.info, April 1, 2016.

[598] "Firebrand cleric of London mosque," CNN, January 20, 2003.

[599] "Profile: Abu Hamza," BBC, January 17, 2003.

[600] "Mosque Raid Arrests," Sky News, January 20, 2003; "Timeline: UK ricin terror probe," CNN, January 23, 2003.

[601] Ibid.

[602] Michael Petrou, "'It's OK to kill non-Muslims': Says Radical Cleric," *Ottawa Citizen*, November 24, 2002.

[603] Ibid.

[604] Simon Mann, "Hatred mongers exploit freedom of speech," *Sydney Morning Herald*, September 22, 2001.

[605] Ibid.

[606] Jon Ronson, *Them: Adventures with Extremists*, Simon & Schuster, 2002, p. 23.

[607] Jon Dougherty, "Muslim leaders pledge to 'transform West,'" World Net Daily, August 13, 2002.

[608] Ibid.

609 Ibid.

610 Ibid.

611 Anton La Guardia, Said Ghazzali, Ohad Gozani, and Sean O'Neill, "British bombers posed as peace activists," Telegraph, May 2, 2003.

612 "Body on Tel Aviv Beach ID'd As Bomber," Associated Press, May 19, 2003.

613 "Radical cleric 'taught' bomb suspects," BBC, May 2, 2003.

614 Ibid.

615 Sarah Lyall, "What Drove 2 Britons to Bomb a Club in Tel Aviv?" New York Times, May 12, 2003.

616 Ibid.

617 Ibid.

618 Ibid.

619 David Bamber, Daniel Foggo and Martin Bentham, "MI5 admits: we let suicide bombers slip through net," Telegraph, May 4, 2003.

620 Sarah Lyall, "What Drove 2 Britons to Bomb a Club in Tel Aviv?"

621 "Cameron: 'Woolwich was a betrayal of Islam,'" ITV News, June 3, 2013.

622 Christopher Caldwell, "Allah Mode.".

623 Jack Montgomery, "UK Govt to 'Resettle Thousands More Refugees Starting Next Year, for Years to Come,'" Breitbart, June 20, 2019.

624 Ibid.

625 Virginia Hale, "UN Refugee Chief Says Europe Must Prepare Systems to Cope with Bigger Migrant Flows," Breitbart, January 25, 2018.

626 Howard Schneider, "For First Time, a Pope Sets Foot in a Mosque," Washington Post, May 7, 2001.

627 "Friday Sermons in Saudi Mosques: Review and Analysis," Middle East Media Research Institute, September 26, 2002.

628 Quentin Hoster, "Faire respecter le confinement dans les banlieues, 'pas une priorité' pour le gouvernement," Valeurs Actuelles, March 25, 2020.

629 Ibid.

630 Neville Chamberlain, *In Search of Peace,* 1939, p. 393; and *Parliamentary Debates, House of Commons,* London, HMSO, 1938, vol. 339, 12th vol. of session 1937–1938, pp. 361–369, 373.

631 Bat Ye'or, "How Europe Became Eurabia."

632 Bat Ye'or, "Eurabia: The Road to Munich."

633 Alexander Mallin and John Parkinson, "Paris Attacks a 'Terrible, Sickening Setback' in ISIS Fight, Obama Says," ABC News, November 16, 2015; "Obama criticises Republicans' anti-migrants stance," Financial Times, November 16, 2015.

634 "Obama criticises Republicans' anti-migrants stance."

635 Donna Rachel Edmunds, "Muslim Countries Refuse to Take A Single Syrian Refugee, Cite Risk of Exposure to Terrorism," Breitbart, September 5, 2015.

636 "Obama criticises Republicans' anti-migrants stance."

637 Ibid.

638 Ibid.

639 Max Brantley, "Gov. Asa Hutchinson: Syrian refugees unwelcome in Arkansas," Arkansas Times, November 16, 2015.

640 Maria Sacchetti and Tracy Jan, "Baker's stance on refugees draws ire of immigration groups," Boston Globe, November 16, 2015.

641 Maria Sacchetti and Tracy Jan, "Baker's stance on refugees draws ire of immigration groups," Boston Globe, November 16, 2015.

642 "Obama criticises Republicans' anti-migrants stance."

643 Ibid.

644 Ibid.

645 Ibid.

646 Ibid.

647 Ryan Teague Beckwith, "President Trump's Remarks on 'Defending Civilization' in Poland," Time, July 6, 2017.

648 "Obama's Speech to the United Nations General Assembly—Text," New York Times, September 25, 2012.

649 "President Trump's Remarks on 'Defending Civilization' in Poland."

650 Ibid.

# INDEX

Made in the USA
Columbia, SC
09 January 2021